Key Issues in Special Education

Considerable challenges can face all those involved in teaching children with special educational needs. Complex policy and legislation, bureaucracy, inspection and limited resources can all seem like difficult obstacles to those seeking to provide effective tuition.

In this accessible and highly practical book, Michael Farrell unpicks and clarifies the role of educational standards in today's schools. Drawing extensively on detailed, real-life case studies, he closely explores such issues as:

- The definition of standards
- Identifying, assessing and providing for special educational needs
- Assessment and benchmarking
- Curriculum provision and target-setting
- The role of the Code of Practice

Special educational needs co-ordinators, senior managers in schools and students completing initial training courses will find this an invaluable resource, which effortlessly simplifies an often complicated process.

Michael Farrell is a freelance educational consultant, and recognised expert in special education. He has written or edited over 30 acclaimed education books.

Key Issues in Special Education

Raising standards of pupils' attainment and achievement

Michael Farrell

Routledge
Taylor & Francis Group

LONDON AND NEW YORK

First published 2005 by Routledge
2 Park Square, Abingdon, Oxon, OX14 4RN
Simultaneously published in the USA and Canada
by Routledge
270 Madison Ave, New York, NY 10016

Routledge is an imprint of the Taylor & Francis Group

© 2005 Michael Farrell

Typeset in Times by
GreenGate Publishing Services, Tonbridge, Kent
Printed and bound in Great Britain by
TJ International Limited, Padstow, Cornwall

British Library Cataloguing in Publication Data
A catalogue record for this book is available from the British Library

Library of Congress Cataloging in Publication Data
Farrell, Michael, 1948–
Key issues in special education / Michael Farrell.
        p. cm.
    Includes bibliographical references and index.
    ISBN 0-415-35423-4 (hardback : alk. paper)–ISBN 0-415-35424-2
(pbk. : alk. paper) 1. Children with disabilities–Education–Great Britain.
2. Special education–Standards–Great Britain. 3. Special education–Great
Britain–Evaluation. I. Title.

LC4036.G7F37 2005
371.9'0941–dc22

                                                    2004021900

This book is dedicated to John Dewhurst
with warm affection.

Contents

Illustrations

Tables

Case studies

The author

Having trained as a teacher and as a research psychologist (Institute of Psychiatry), Michael Farrell taught pupils ranging from very able to those with profound and multiple learning difficulties. He has worked as a head teacher, a lecturer at the London University Institute of Education and as an LEA inspector for special education. After managing a national psychological project at City University he directed a project for the then Department for Education and Employment, developing materials and course structures for teacher education. He is currently a special education consultant with local education authorities, schools, voluntary organisations, universities and others, both in Britain and abroad. Author of many articles on education and psychology, he has also edited educational books. Among his several other recent publications are:

Key Issues for Primary Schools (Routledge 2000)
Key Issues for Secondary Schools (Routledge 2001)
Understanding Special Educational Needs: A Guide for Student Teachers (RoutledgeFalmer 2003)

Acknowledgements

I am grateful to the following colleagues for help with the various chapters:

Chapter 2: Bridget Jones, Regional Facilitator, West Midlands SEN Regional Partnership for drawing my attention to the work of the Partnership and 14 LEAs in developing jointly agreed criteria for statutory assessment of SEN. Keith Stapylton, Head of Special Educational Needs, Bracknell Forest LEA, for providing information used in the case study and for commenting on the chapter.

Chapter 3: Mary Kuhn, Regional Facilitator, London SEN Regional Partnership, for information used in the case study and comments on the case study.

Chapter 4: Kevan Thompson, Lancashire LEA, for comments on this chapter. Jean Cook, Head teacher, Pear Tree School, Lancashire for help with the case study.

Chapter 6: Roger Norgate, Senior Consultant Educational Psychologist, Hampshire LEA, for comments on the case study.

Chapter 7: Paul Fisher, Head of Education Finance and Information and Communication Technology Service, Norfolk LEA, for information for the case study.

Chapter 8: Pat Graham, Regional Facilitator, East Midland Regional Partnership, for help contacting LEAs.

Angela Cole, Derby LEA, for help contacting schools.

Sue Hales, SENCO, Bishop Lonsdale Church of England (Aided) Primary School and Nursery, Derby for providing the information for the case study.

Introduction

In this book, I shall take the advice of the king in *Alice in Wonderland*. I shall begin at the beginning, go on until I reach the end, then stop. But there was a precursor to the present volume, namely, *Standards and Special Educational Needs: The Importance of Standards of Pupil Achievement* published by Continuum in 2001. The generous reception of that book led me to conclude that its theme was tapping a strong vein of interest and concern among its many readers. This theme essentially was that a key focus for pupils with SEN should be raising standards of pupil attainment and achievement in curriculum subjects and raising standards of pupil achievement in personal, social and emotional development.

This was preferable to the vague and perhaps condescending approach of trying to meet supposed needs or the vacuousness of 'celebrating diversity'. The present book therefore continues and further develops this theme.

Readers of the book

The book is intended for all those with an interest in special education, for example:

- head teachers and deputy/assistant head teachers, especially those studying educational leadership and management
- senior teachers
- special education co-ordinators (SENCOs)
- parents
- governors and managers
- education advisers and inspectors/consultants
- local government officers including educational psychologists
- teaching assistants
- teachers in training and those who work with them

- newly qualified teachers and those supporting them
- teachers and others pursuing continuing professional development
- students on professional courses for the health and social services requiring a perspective on SEN
- health and social service professionals.

The format and uses of the book

The book comprises ten chapters, a bibliography and an index. Each chapter has its own introduction, headed sections and a summary/conclusion, and some include case studies to further illustrate the approach and to show how it works in practice.

I seek to illustrate the importance in special education of raising standards of pupils' attainment and achievement (the progress made and the standards reached by pupils, taking into account their apparent capabilities). An aspect of this is the standard of attainment reached by the pupil in areas of the curriculum (such as speaking and listening, literacy and numeracy), as well as the pupil's level of achievement in personal, social and emotional development.

This focus on standards involves considering legislation, policies, procedure and practice. The book works through various aspects of special education to show the importance of a pupil's attainment and achievement, opportunities to further develop them and the challenges in seeking to do so. These aspects of special education embrace:

- definitions of special educational needs (SEN) and related terms, particularly in legislation
- the assessment and identification of SEN and types of SEN
- target-setting, benchmarking and value-added approaches
- personal and social development and behaviour in relation to target-setting
- inclusion as it relates to SEN
- special education funding at both local and national levels
- the use of data on the attainment, achievement and progress of pupils with SEN (in interaction with the pupil's gender, ethnicity and other factors)
- the use of SEN attainment, achievement and progress data in relation to school provision (quality of teaching and learning, school organisation and pupil grouping; professional support, parents and the community)
- the role of the special school.

The geographical focus

In order to follow through the implications of this approach of focusing on raising standards in a coherent way, the system that I consider is that in England at the time of writing. This enables one to consider together related topics including legislation, government guidance, policies, a range of approaches used in schools and possibilities for further developing the focus on pupils' standards.

However, much of what the book has to say should interest educators and others in other English-speaking, developed countries who may wish to consider the implications of the ideas and approaches covered in the book and their application to their own country. These countries include Wales, Scotland, Northern Ireland, Republic of Ireland, the United States of America, Canada, Australia and New Zealand.

Readers from countries other than England could follow through the approach of this book, should they wish, adapting it to their own legislative procedures, policies and practices as necessary. Some issues such as inclusion and the quality of teaching and learning are common to many countries.

Standards, standards, standards

Standards of various kinds have assumed increasing importance in the English education system in recent decades. Among these are standards developed by the Teacher Training Agency which include the following. The *National Standards for Special Educational Needs Co-ordinators* concerns the core purpose of the SENCO, key outcomes of SEN co-ordination, professional knowledge and understanding, skills and attributes, and key areas of SEN co-ordination (Teacher Training Agency 1998).

The *National SEN Specialist Standards* aims to help the school identify training and development needs relating to the effective teaching of pupils with severe and/or complex SEN. It concerns head teachers and teachers in mainstream schools; teachers and managers of special classes and units in mainstream schools; staff in special schools and pupil referral units; and teachers and managers in support services (Teacher Training Agency 1999).

The *Professional Standards for Qualified Teacher Status* (Teacher Training Agency 2002a) sets out the values, knowledge, understanding and teaching that must be demonstrated for a trainee teacher to be awarded qualified teacher status (QTS).

The *Induction Standards for Newly Qualified Teachers* (Teacher Training Agency 2002b) lays down similar requirements that must be met if a newly qualified teacher (NQT) is to complete the induction process successfully. (The book, *Understanding Special Educational Needs: A Guide for Student Teachers* [Farrell 2003a], explores and develops the SEN implications of the *QTS Standards* and *Induction Standards*.)

In the *Professional Standards for Higher Level Teaching Assistants* (Teacher Training Agency 2003), higher level teaching assistants are expected to demonstrate certain professional values and practice; knowledge and understanding; and teaching and learning activities.

The present book is concerned with standards of pupil attainment, standards of pupil achievement and pupil progress, all of which are more precisely defined in Chapter 1, 'Defining special educational needs'. Whatever one's view concerning standards for head teachers, teachers, specialist teachers and others, the standards of attainment and achievement of pupils and the progress that they make cannot be ignored or marginalised. They are at the heart of education. Not to give them due regard would be like thinking that a hospital's function to try to make people better was an optional extra to be considered seriously only when patients had been made to feel welcome.

National strategies to raise standards of attainment

It would be odd to anticipate finding many national strategies that do not intend to raise standards of attainment of pupils, if one accepts that the main purpose of schools is to enable teaching and learning and that pupils' attainment is an indicator of the effectiveness of teaching and learning. For example, *Excellence and Enjoyment: A Strategy for Primary Schools* (DfES 2003b) seeks to pair enjoyment with raising standards, stating:

> We want schools to continue to focus on raising standards while not being afraid to combine that with making learning fun.
>
> (ibid., p. 4, executive summary)

For pupils with SEN, the strategy aims to encourage the improvement of value-added measures:

> ... so that schools get credit for the performance of all children, including children working below the level of the tests, many of whom have special educational needs.
>
> (ibid., p. 7)

With regard to the reporting of results of children with SEN, the report indicates:

> It is right that children with special educational needs should have their achievements recognised, and that they are not left out of our drive to improve standards for all.
>
> (ibid., pp. 23–4)

In the *Key Stage 3 National Strategy* (DfES 2002), the aims of the strategy are said to be to:

> ... raise the standards achieved by 11 to 14 year olds by transforming approaches to teaching and learning.
>
> (ibid., p. 1)

The strategy 'Excellence in Cities' is described in a report by the Office for Standards in Education (2003) as:

> ... another of the government's central initiatives aimed at raising educational standards and promoting social inclusion in major cities and in areas that face similar problems to those faced in the inner cities.
>
> (ibid., p. 6)

Similarly, Education Action Zones are described as having been set up:

> ... to tackle problems of underachievement and social exclusion in disadvantaged areas by devising innovative methods and strategies that would involve disaffected pupils more fully in education and improve their academic performance.
>
> (ibid., p. 5)

To strive to raise the standards of pupils' attainment and achievement is not a hindrance that somehow gets in the way of learning. Better attainment and achievement are the essential indications that learning is taking place. Therefore, it is important to push for better attainment in all pupils. To settle for merely meeting the supposed needs of pupils with SEN runs the risk of offering them second best.

Chapter 1

Defining special educational needs

Introduction

This chapter seeks to elucidate terms. I explain what I mean by standards of pupil attainment, pupil achievement and progress, first in general and then with particular reference to pupils with special educational needs (SEN). After considering, in the context of English legislation, different legal definitions of 'disability', I examine the legal definition of SEN in the Education Act 1996, which includes definitions both of 'disability' and of 'difficulty in learning'. The chapter then relates the legal definition of SEN to standards of pupil attainment and progress.

I indicate how a consideration of standards pupil attainment and progress helps distinguish pupils with SEN from pupils for whom English is an additional language, pupils with low attainments because of poor educational opportunities, and very able pupils. The chapter examines why it is important that SEN is defined. Finally, I examine how many pupils are believed to need special educational provision, considering the issue of manageability in some schools.

Standards of pupil attainment, standards of pupil achievement and progress

In this section, I explain what I mean by standards of attainment, standards of achievement and progress. An attempt was made to distinguish attainment and achievement in the Office for Standards in Education *Handbooks* (OfSTED 2003a, 2003b, 2003c). But the use of the two terms is not always consistent and sometimes the documents speak confusingly of 'standards achieved' before going on to discuss standards of attainment as well as standards of achievement (e.g. OfSTED 2003b, p. 43). However, a useful distinction can be drawn between attainment and achievement, even if it is easy to slip from one to the other. The following examples draw on the *Handbook for Inspecting Secondary Schools* (OfSTED 2003b), but the approach is similar for primary schools, special schools and pupil referral units.

Standards of *attainment* refer to the standards that pupils reach in curriculum subjects such as English, mathematics and science in terms of national comparisons with other pupils of the same age. Accordingly, the *Handbook for Inspecting Secondary Schools* states that 'Where national assessments, tests and examinations apply to pupils at the school, inspectors should interpret the results and trends so that parents and others can understand what the data mean' (OfSTED 2003b, p. 43).

Standards of *achievement* concern the standards that pupils reach when their capabilities and their progress have been taken into consideration and they can involve a judgement about whether these standards are as high as they should be. They apply not only to curriculum subjects but also to the pupils' attitudes to learning and aspects of development. The *Handbook for Inspecting Secondary Schools* states that:

> The main judgements concern whether the achievements of the pupils are as high as they should be, taking into account their capabilities and the progress they have made in the school. Achievements include pupils' knowledge, skills and understanding gained through the subjects of the curriculum, and the attitudes, values, and other aspects of personal development fostered by the school.
>
> (OfSTED 2003b, p. 43)

One reason that achievement rather than attainment is considered to apply to personal development is that it is difficult to speak of attainment in terms of national levels in connection with, for example, behaviour or self-esteem. However, even in assessing personal development, there are attempts to provide consistency and an element of standardisation. These are explored in a later chapter.

The notion of capability (like 'potential') is problematic because one has to be careful not to underestimate or overestimate what a child might be capable of. If the child's prior learning and the rate of learning of other children are taken into account, this can sharpen the use of the term.

But why is the distinction between attainment and achievement important? Pupils in a secondary school may be reaching high levels of *attainment* in examinations at age 16 when compared with pupils of the same age nationally. But it may reasonably be expected that they should have done better due, for example, to the very high standards of attainment they had at the start of secondary school (their prior attainment). It may be, therefore, that their standards of *achievement* are too low. The judgement about attainment, it will be seen, takes into account their 'capability' (including what they can already do) and their progress.

The difference between attainment and achievement is helpful also when applied to pupils with SEN. Consider an example of a primary school that educates pupils with SEN in the form of severe speech or communication difficulties. In the national assessments of speaking and listening, the pupils reach standards much lower than those of pupils of the same age nationally as reflected in end of key stage standard assessment tests and tasks. Their standards of attainment are low.

The question then is, should the school be expected to do better? The answer to this will depend on various factors. Firstly, without setting too low (or too high) aspirations for the pupils with SEN, a judgement will have to be made about the pupils' 'capability'. This will be informed by what they could already do earlier in their school career. Also, the progress that they have made in school will be assessed. This may be judged perhaps taking into account the views of speech and language therapists, teachers, the pupil, parents and others as being for example poor, satisfactory, or good. This will lead to a judgement about whether the pupils' standards of achievement are high enough. Further refinements can be made to the judgements about standards of achievement by comparing the progress of pupils with severe speech and communication difficulties with that of other pupils with similar difficulties (perhaps in another school) starting from a similar 'baseline'. Such approaches are discussed later in the book.

As has already been indicated, it is important to remember that standards of pupil achievement apply not only to subjects of the curriculum but also to personal development. When the OfSTED framework refers to 'standards' for example, it addresses the questions, 'How high are the standards achieved in the areas of learning and subjects and courses of the curriculum?' but also, 'How well are the pupils' attitudes, values and other personal qualities developed?' (e.g. OfSTED 2003b, p. 44 and p. 56).

In looking at pupils' standards of attainment, standards of achievement, and progress, we have already begun to touch on issues concerning SEN. It is now necessary to retrace our steps a little and consider in more detail what SEN is taken to mean in current legislation in England.

Legal definitions of disability in England

There are (different) definitions of disability in the Children Act 1989, the Disability Discrimination Act 1995 and the Education Act 1996. This section considers the definitions of disability in the first two Acts.

The Children Act 1989 (England and Wales) section 17 describes children with disabilities within a wider context of children 'in need' which allows eligibility for certain support and services from the local authority. A child is 'in need' if:

a   he/she is unlikely to achieve or maintain, or to have the opportunity of achieving or maintaining a reasonable standard of health or development without the provision for him/her of services by a local authority under this [Part] of the Act;

b   his/her health or development is likely to be significantly impaired, or further impaired, without the provision for him/her of such services

c   he/she is disabled.

'Development' refers to physical, intellectual, emotional, social or behavioural development while 'health' encompasses physical and mental health. The Act states that:

> A child is disabled if he is blind, deaf or dumb or suffers from mental disorder of any kind or is substantially and permanently handicapped by illness, injury or congenital deformity or other such disability as may be prescribed.

The Disability Discrimination Act 1995 defines a disabled person as someone who has:

> … a physical or mental impairment which has a substantial and long term adverse effect on his ability to carry out normal day-to-day activities.

The term 'physical or mental impairment' includes sensory impairments such as those affecting sight or hearing; learning difficulties and clinically well-recognised mental illness.

The legal definition of SEN in England

Having looked at the definitions of disability in the Children Act 1989 and in the Disability Discrimination Act 1995, I now consider the Education Act 1996. This includes a further definition of 'disability' and also a definition of 'difficulty in learning', both of which are then related to 'learning difficulty' and 'special educational need' (Education Act 1996, section 312).

The term special educational needs came to be commonly employed in England following its use in the 'Warnock Report' (DES 1978, Passim.). Before then it was more usual to refer to categories of 'handicap' set under regulations following the Education Act 1944, namely: blind; partially sighted; deaf; partially deaf; delicate; diabetic; educationally subnormal; epileptic; maladjusted; physically handicapped, and speech defect. Following the 'Warnock Report', the Education Act 1981 replaced the previous categories of handicap with a broader definition of SEN. Among other things, the shift to SEN helped indicate that the previous 'handicapping conditions' were to be seen in relation to learning. They were no longer categories carrying with them the possible connotations that development was arrested and that the child's difficulties or disabilities were fixed or exclusively within the child.

The notion of SEN has been carried forward into subsequent legislation including the Education Act 1996 where the definition is that:

> a child has special educational needs ... if he has a learning difficulty which calls for special educational provision to be made for him
>
> (Education Act 1996, section 312)

Defining 'learning difficulty', the Act states that a child has a learning difficulty if:

a   he has a significantly greater difficulty in learning than the majority of children of his age

b   he has a disability which either prevents or hinders him from making use of educational facilities of a kind generally provided for children of his age in schools within the area of the local education authority

c   he is under the age of five and is, or would be if special educational provision were not made for him, likely to fall within paragraph (a) and (b) when of, or over that age

(Education Act 1996, section 312 (2))

'Special educational provision' means:

a   for a child of two or over, educational provision which is additional to, or otherwise different from, the educational provision made generally for children of their age in schools maintained by the LEA, other than special schools, in the area

b   for children under two, educational provision of any kind.

(Education Act 1996, section 312).

'Difficulty in learning' and 'learning difficulty' in relation to standards of pupil attainment

'Difficulty in learning' and 'learning difficulty'

There is a nested structure to the legal definition of SEN. It will be seen from the legal definition that a child may have a 'difficulty in learning' but not a 'learning difficulty'. This arises because the 'difficulty in learning' may not be a 'significantly greater difficulty in learning than the majority of children of his age' (Education Act 1996 section 312 (2)).

Also, a child may have a 'learning difficulty' but not a 'special educational need'. This is because the child's learning difficulty may not call for 'special educational provision to be made for him' (ibid.). This special educational provision, it will be remembered, is educational provision which is 'additional to, or otherwise different from, the educational provision made generally for children of their age in schools maintained by the LEA, other than special schools, in the area' (ibid.).

So a child may have a 'difficulty in learning' but not a 'learning difficulty' and may have a 'learning difficulty' but not a 'special educational need'. Only when a child has a 'difficulty in learning' which constitutes a 'learning difficulty' which calls for special educational provision to be made, does the child have a SEN. In this case, the SEN may be for example 'specific learning difficulty', 'moderate learning difficulty', 'severe learning difficulty' or 'profound and multiple learning difficulty'. It will be seen that such SENs equate with and are partly defined according to attainment and progress. For example, a child with moderate learning difficulty will have lower attainments than other children of the same age and will have made slower progress.

'Disability' and 'learning difficulty' in relation to standards of pupil attainment

The nested nature of the definition of SEN applies to disability (e.g. hearing impairment; visual impairment; multi-sensory impairment; physical difficulties) as well as to difficulty in learning. A child may have a 'disability' but not a 'learning difficulty'. This is because the disability may not either prevent or hinder him 'from making use of educational facilities of a kind generally provided for children of his age in schools within the area of the local education authority' (Education Act 1996, section 312).

Similarly the child can have a 'learning difficulty' brought about by a 'disability' but not have a SEN. This is because the child's learning difficulty does not call for 'special educational provision to be made for him'. Special education provision is, educational provision which is 'additional to, or otherwise different from, the educational provision made generally for children of their age in schools maintained by the LEA, other than special schools, in the area' (ibid.).

So a child may have a 'disability' but not a 'learning difficulty' and may have a 'learning difficulty' but not a 'special educational need'. Only when a child has a 'disability' constituting a 'learning difficulty' calling for special educational provision to be made, does the child have a SEN.

Disability in relation to SEN does not relate to standards of attainment and progress in the same way that 'difficulty in learning' leading to 'learning difficulty' does. Disability such as blindness does not equate with (and is not partly defined by) lower attainment and slower progress than age average in curriculum areas or in personal, social and behavioural development. In the case of disability, the learning difficulty that leads to a SEN concerns a physical impairment leading to a difficulty in gaining access to learning and the curriculum.

However, standards of attainment and progress still play a central role. To the extent that educational provision is appropriate for a pupil with a disability, the pupil can be expected to make faster progress and attain a higher level than would be the case otherwise. In other words, faster progress and a higher standard of attainment for a disabled pupil is an indication that the educational provision is suitable.

Relationship between 'difficulty in learning' and 'disability'

The above discussion has considered separately 'difficulty in learning' (leading to learning difficulty and a SEN) and 'disability' (leading to learning difficulty and a SEN).

However, 'difficulty in learning' and 'disability' cannot always be neatly separated. For example, a child with speech or communication problems may have these because of an apparent difficulty in learning and processing language or because of a physical deficit in the formation of the mouth or tongue. Also, a child with profound and multiple learning difficulties (PMLD) may have profound learning difficulties but also a disability such as hearing impairment or visual impairment.

However, the earlier discussion has, it is hoped, indicated an important distinction in the legal definition and a real distinction that can be made between 'difficulty in learning' and 'disability' as they concern SEN. For a broad overview of education legislation in England and Wales see Farrell *et al.*(1995). For an overview of special education legislation particularly in England, see Farrell (2003b).

Avoiding potential confusion between SEN and other factors

Potential confusion

It is possible to confuse evidence that a pupil has SEN with evidence having other educational implications regarding:

- pupils who have English as an additional language
- pupils with low attainments because of poor educational opportunities and
- pupils who are very able.

Below, I indicate how necessary distinctions can be made between pupils with SEN and these other pupils by taking account of standards of pupils' attainment and progress.

Pupils who have English as an additional language

Children for whom English is an additional language may be incorrectly considered as having SEN if only levels of attainment are taken into account and not rate of progress. A pupil for whom English is an additional language may have low attainment in literacy in English. But this may not be because of slow progress, learning difficulty and SEN. It may be because the child has not had much exposure to learning English.

Among indications that the child does not have difficulties in learning (still less learning difficulty or SEN), would be that his/her progress in learning English is satisfactory or better. Also, in other subjects in which English is not as central as it is in literacy, he/she may make satisfactory or better progress. For example, with necessary language translation, he/she makes satisfactory progress in mathematics. If a child simply has low attainment in English, but learns at a satisfactory rate or better, the child does not have SEN.

Pupils with low attainment because of poor educational opportunities

Teachers and others exercise caution when making a judgement that a very young child has SEN because of low attainment, perhaps indicated by baseline assessment. Low attainment may be an indication that a child has had impoverished experiences of learning at home. At school, the child may make satisfactory or better progress in learning, indicating that he/she does not have difficulties in learning (still less learning difficulties or SEN).

However, it may be that poor educational opportunities exerienced by a child before entering school has led not just to low attainment in comparison with others but has also contributed to slower progress than other children. The child's capacity to learn, to use thinking skills, and to explore his/her environment may have been inhibited and discouraged to an extent that progress is slow. In such a case, the two concomitants of 'difficulty in learning' and 'learning difficulty' (that is low attainment and slow progress) may well be apparent. The child may then be considered to have SEN. The main issue is that it cannot always be assumed that, because a child enters school attaining a lower level than other children, he/she will not rapidly progress and catch up. This is a subtle and important judgement for teachers and others to make.

Very able pupils

If a pupil with SEN relating to 'learning difficulties' brought about by 'difficulties in learning' can be defined in terms of slow progress and low attainment, then a very able pupil is one making rapid progress and attaining a high level. Therefore a pupil who is very able would not, by definition, be considered as having SEN. Very able pupils may have particular learning 'needs', but they do not have SEN.

Of course, a pupil may be very able in one aspect of the curriculum such as physical education, but have difficulties in relation to another area of learning such as literacy, perhaps leading to a judgement that he has a SEN such as dyslexia. Furthermore, a pupil may be very able in some school subjects but have behavioural, emotional and social difficulties constituting a SEN. Occasionally, a pupil with a SEN such as autism may have a particular skill in an area of learning such as drawing or music at a level that is higher than age average.

Why SEN is defined

Having looked at how SEN is defined and at the role of standards of attainment and progress in this, I now turn to the question of why SEN should be defined and identified at all.

Special education is a moral response to children considered to 'have' SEN. It is justified by the particular circumstances of the pupil (his or her 'need'). This special provision is preferential educational provision which is, 'additional to, or otherwise different from, the educational provision made generally for children of their age in schools maintained by the LEA, other than special schools, in the area' (Education Act 1996, section 312).

In practice the provision is usually 'additional to' what is provided as standard. A guidance document giving descriptions of types of SEN to help schools and LEAs to record pupils' needs in the Pupil Level Annual Schools Census specifies the nature of provision clearly. For example, pupils considered as having 'moderate learning difficulty' are described and the guidance then advises, 'They should only be recorded as MLD if *additional* educational provision is being made to help them access the curriculum' (DfES 2003a, p. 3, italics added).

The measures taken might involve closer individual monitoring of progress through such means as Individual Education Plans, individualised approaches to teaching and learning or the provision of equipment. It is not possible (nor is it appropriate or necessary) to make this provision for all pupils, so it is necessary to identify which pupils require the additional support to benefit more fully from their education. This is why a special educational need is defined.

How many pupils should receive special educational provision?

An attempt to estimate percentages

In Britain in the 1970s, the 'Warnock Report' (DES 1978) not only advised that the term 'special educational needs' should replace the former 'categories of handicap' but also that the new term should be much broader and apply to more children. The report indicated that a reasonable proportion of pupils to consider as having SEN would be about one child in six or just below 17 per cent at any one time. This percentage of pupils would be considered as benefiting from some form of special education. Around one child in five pupils or about 20 per cent would require some form of special education at some time in their school career. In short, the committee attempted to give an indication of the proportion of pupils appropriate to be considered as having a SEN.

Such a percentage estimate may be useful for policy purposes if the numbers concerned are very large such as the school pupil population of the whole of England. In such a context, it is meaningful to speak of about 17 per cent of pupils 'having' SEN. But if the population is small, such as that of an individual school, it is less likely that a percentage will be a useful guide to SEN.

Why individual schools cannot assume a certain percentage of pupils with SEN

The limitations of relying on percentages in individual schools may be illustrated by taking an example of a type of SEN, that of the specific learning difficulty dyslexia manifesting itself as difficulty with reading (and perhaps writing and spelling). Assume it was accepted that in a country as a whole such pupils received special educational provision (for example involving individual reading programmes, lap-top computers and so on). Then it would make sense to speak of this proportion of pupils, say 5 per cent of the pupil population, receiving special education and having SEN. It would be accepted that not every school with a hundred pupils would necessarily have 5 with reading and related difficulties. Some such schools might have fewer while others might have more.

It would be wrong if one of the schools with fewer than 5 per cent of pupils with reading and related difficulties claimed to have 5 per cent (for example because extra funds were allocated for providing for them), simply because statistically they could have 5 per cent. The determining criterion would be that the reading and related difficulty would be as clearly defined as possible and if a school clearly had less than 5 per cent of such pupils, then any protestation that they had more or any claim for funding would be dismissed. Objective criteria would discourage abuse of the funding system.

Why the term 'peers' applies to national data and not to pupils in an individual school

There is a variation of the misunderstanding about percentages explained above. A school with, for example, few pupils with reading difficulties might claim that the proportion of pupils with reading and related difficulties that were thought to apply nationally still ought to apply to it as an individual school despite any local criteria. It might argue that, although its pupils did not have the degree of reading difficulties as severe as any existing LEA criteria required, nevertheless, it did have pupils who were behind other pupils in the school. Therefore, in the context of the school, it did have pupils who had difficulties in learning greater than their peers. What the school is ignoring in its claim is that 'peers' refers to pupils nationally, not to those in individual schools.

To illustrate the inappropriateness and unfairness of such a school claim, consider that the same argument could be used by a selective school for very able pupils all achieving far above the age average for pupils nationally in literacy. It could claim that 5 per cent of its pupils (or an even higher percentage) had SEN related to reading because they were behind other pupils in the school. In relation to the fair allocation of funds in an LEA, such a school-context approach would lead to funds being spuriously allocated for 'SEN' where they were least needed rather than to where they were most needed.

Using criteria for SEN and retaining manageability

Criteria then should determine SEN rather than the vagaries of individual school context. Therefore, teachers, LEA officers, parents and others have to decide and agree as carefully as they can, within the parameters of legislation, what they mean by SEN and what the types of SEN are. They have to decide who falls into the group of pupils considered to have SEN and who does not, although there will inevitably be debate about pupils on the fringes of the definition of SEN and about interpretation. These criteria are often related to standards of pupil attainment (in the case of 'difficulty in learning' leading to 'learning difficulty' and SEN) or they may be based on measurable criteria (as in the instance of a disability like hearing impairment).

To define SEN according to criteria relating to standards of pupil attainment raises the question of manageability. It has already been indicated that the distribution of pupils with SEN may not be similar across different schools. To the extent that the additional or different provision for pupils with SEN involves individualised work and monitoring (as reflected for example in Individual Education Plans), the provision is manageable only with a small percentage of pupils in any one school.

It is more difficult where a school, according to the agreed criteria, has a high percentage of pupils with SEN, say above 20 per cent. A point is reached where the school can no longer reasonably keep track of the individualised planning, provision and monitoring, and there is a danger that chasing up and maintaining documentation will begin to take precedence over the education of pupils.

One approach for a mainstream school is to concentrate on a manageable percentage of pupils with the most severe SEN and to seek to provide for other pupils with SEN through whole school strategies, including multi-professional approaches. This would be assisted if equitable funding were allocated to the school according to the number of pupils it has with SEN so long as these were determined according to locally agreed criteria.

A parallel may be drawn with a special school. The special school benefits from factors such as small class sizes and a very favourable teacher–pupil ratio, special resources throughout the school and specially trained and experienced staff. Therefore such schools are able to provide education for pupils, all of whom have severe SEN. Individual Education Plans may be developed only for those children who require something additional to or different from what the school already provides for all pupils. To the extent that a mainstream school with a high percentage of pupils with (less severe) SEN can offer school-wide or group focused provision that supports the SEN, fewer individual approaches are likely to be needed. The school is still legally giving 'special educational provision' to the extent that it is offering something 'additional to or otherwise different from' that which is generally provided in other local schools in the LEA area, in this example, more extensive and intensive multi-professional support.

Summary/conclusion

The aspects of the legal definition of SEN in the Education Act 1996 can be understood in relation to standards of pupils' attainment and progress. SEN related to 'learning difficulty' brought about by 'difficulty in learning' are in part defined in relation to standards of pupils' attainment and progress. The effectiveness of provision for pupils with SEN related to 'learning difficulty' arising from a disability may be evaluated according to the attainment and progress of these pupils. Definitions of types of SEN are informed by attainment and progress.

Pupils' attainment and progress help distinguish pupils with SEN from pupils for whom English is an additional language; pupils with low attainments because of poor educational opportunities; and very able pupils. If special education is understood as a moral response involving preferential provision to pupils with SEN, it is important that SEN is clearly defined. The definition should be agreed by LEA officers, parents and all schools in a local area to avoid abuses of funding by local schools inventing their own definitions.

Thinking points

Readers may wish to consider:

- the degree to which a shared understanding of an agreed definition of SEN is important
- the extent to which in your LEA or school, such a definition has been agreed by LEA officers, parents, schools and others.

Key text

Farrell, M. (2003) *The Special Education Handbook* (3rd edition), London: David Fulton Publishers

The book provides entries on 'difficulty in learning', 'disability', 'learning difficulty', special educational need' and 'special education'. Its appendices cover selected legislation, reports and consultative documents from the time of the 'Warnock Report' to the present day; selected regulations from 1981; and selected circulars and circular letters from 1981 and the Special Educational Needs Code of Practice 1994 and 2001. Included are summaries of the Children Act 1999, the Disability Discrimination Act 1995, and the Special Educational Needs and Disability Act 2001.

Chapter 2

How types of SEN and LEA criteria relate to pupils' standards and progress

Introduction

There is not always universal agreement over SEN issues, but I will maintain in this chapter that it is necessary to seek the support of parents, schools, LEA officers and others as to what is meant by different types of SEN. Firstly I will examine the definitions of types of SEN provided in the Pupil Level Annual School Census (PLASC) guidance (DfES 2003a) in relation to pupils' attainment and progress. The chapter argues that criteria are necessary to refine definitions of SEN and looks at how these relate to standards of pupil attainment and progress. A case study illustrates LEA criteria (thresholds) for the statutory assessment of SEN.

Types of SEN

An understanding of the definition of SEN set out in the Education Act 1996, and which was examined in Chapter 1, may be supplemented by the details given in the *Special Educational Needs Code of Practice* (Department for Education and Skills, 2001a) (hereafter the *Code*). In Chapter 7 of the *Code*, broad areas of SEN are identified, and it is indicated that they are not rigid and that there may be a considerable degree of overlap between them. These areas are:

- cognition and learning
- behaviour, emotional and social development
- communication and interaction; and
- sensory or physical.

(7.52)

The Department for Education and Skills (2003a) defined categories of SEN to help local education authorities complete the Pupil Level Annual

School Census (PLASC) returns. Schools and LEAs are asked to record the main type of need for pupils with a statement of SEN or for whom provision is being made at Early Years Action Plus or School Action Plus. Pupils at Early Years Action and at School Action are recorded for the census but not in terms of the type of SEN. The guidance asks schools to select the 'main disability or difficulty' from a list which is related to the broad areas of SEN in the *Code*.

These types of SEN are also used in Office for Standards in Education documents such as the 'Notes of Guidance' for completing forms S1 and S2 relating to school inspection (Office for Standards in Education 2003d, p. 4). Each of these types will now be considered in relation to standards of pupil attainment and progress.

Cognition and learning needs, and attainment and progress

Cognition and learning needs comprise specific learning difficulties, moderate learning difficulties, severe learning difficulties, and profound and multiple learning difficulties.

Specific learning difficulties

Specific learning difficulties are usually taken to comprise dyslexia, dyspraxia and dyscalculia.

Below I consider mainly dyslexia in relation to attainment and progress, then briefly touch on dyscalculia and dyspraxia. This is because many of the points raised about dyslexia (such as the potential difficulty with discrepancy approaches) apply also to dyscalculia and dyspraxia and are not repeated.

DYSLEXIA

Dyslexia is characterised by difficulties with reading and spelling. These difficulties are, as Peer and Reid indicate, 'readily observable characteristics of dyslexia' (Peer and Reid 2003, p. 9). Other children have difficulties with reading and spelling but are not dyslexic. There are other factors that are considered to help identify a child with dyslexia and these are related to reading, spelling, writing, memory, co-ordination, organisational difficulties, information processing, phonological difficulties, visual difficulties and discrepancies in attainment in different areas of the curriculum (ibid., pp. 9–13). Nonetheless, central to the problem of dyslexia are difficulties with reading, writing or spelling. Accordingly, the description of dyslexia in the guidance, *Data Collection by Type of Special Educational Needs* (DfES 2003a) says of these pupils, 'Pupils with dyslexia have a marked and persistent difficulty in learning to read, write and spell, despite progress in other areas' (ibid, p. 3).

It would be odd to be told that a child was considered to have dyslexia while the evidence showed that he attained the same level in reading, writing and spelling as his peers. There is a proviso here however. It is possible that the child with dyslexia may just be able to attain at age-appropriate levels in writing, for example, but only because he spends an inordinate amount of time on written homework. To produce the same amount of written homework of the same quality as others might take him two or three times as long because of difficulties with writing. This difficulty (in pace) would be evident in any timed writing task. The pupil with dyslexia would perform at a level far below age average given the same amount of time as children of his age to complete the task. The same would apply to assessments of reading and spelling.

If a child could read, write and spell at age-average levels, and take the same time that other children take to complete related tasks, then it would be strange to say that he had a difficulty with reading, writing and spelling. It is evident therefore that the definition of dyslexia is related to slow progress and low attainment in reading, writing and spelling (particularly under timed conditions).

This should help to explain why it is important to avoid confusion when considering any discrepancy in the view of dyslexia (where there are discrepancies between attainment in different school subjects indicating a specific learning difficulty). Such a view needs to specify that the child is also behind age-average attainment (in timed conditions) in reading, writing or spelling.

Consider a case where a discrepancy arises where a pupil attains the same as other pupils of the same age in reading, writing and spelling under timed conditions. He is assumed to be able to do better because of a discrepancy between the literacy performance and a high intelligence quotient or because he does very well in other subjects that are not so dependent on literacy. In this case, the pupil would not have a SEN because there is no evidence for a greater 'difficulty in learning' in literacy than other pupils of the same age (still less evidence for a 'learning difficulty' or a SEN). It would be equally valid to argue that the pupil was very able because, as well as attaining in normal conditions at age-average levels in literacy, he was attaining much higher than might be expected in other subjects.

DYSCALCULIA

Guidance on the 'types' of SEN state that 'Pupils with dyscalculia have difficulty in acquiring mathematical skills' (DfES 2003a, p. 3). Following the same argument presented above for dyslexia, I suggest this implies the child progressing more slowly than children of the same age in mathematics and having lower attainment in mathematics.

DYSPRAXIA

According to the guidance on the 'types' of SEN, for pupils with dyspraxia, 'Gross and fine motor skills are hard to learn and difficult to retain and generalise' (DfES 2003, p. 3). Also, 'Pupils may have poor balance and co-ordination and may be hesitant in many actions ...' (ibid., p. 3). Their 'articulation may be immature and their language late to develop' and they 'may also have poor awareness of body position and poor social skills' (ibid., p. 3). Again I suggest that this can translate into the child progressing more slowly than children of the same age in terms of co-ordination and achieving less well. This may also apply, for some children, to balance, articulation, body awareness and social skills.

Moderate learning difficulties

In terms of attainment, a child with moderate learning difficulties (MLD) will be by definition considerably behind other children of the same age who do not have a difficulty in learning. The child's progress in learning will be slow and this will lead to low standards of attainment. This is illustrated if we imagine a discussion in which one person states that a child has MLD. When asked for evidence of these difficulties, he replies that the child attains the same level as other children of the same age. Such a response would strike the listener as nonsensical. The low attainment and slow progress are part of what it means to say that a child has MLD. (The same applies to a greater degree when one considers severe learning difficulty and profound and multiple learning difficulty.)

The description of moderate learning difficulties in the guidance *Data Collection by Types of Special Educational Needs* includes that these pupils '... will have attainments significantly below expected levels in most areas of the curriculum, despite appropriate interventions (DfES 2003a, p. 3).

Severe learning difficulty

The guidance says of pupils with severe learning difficulties that, 'Their attainments may be within the upper P scale range (P4–P8) for much of their school careers (that is, below level 1 of the National Curriculum' (DfES 2003a, p. 3).

To remind readers of the levels indicated in such a description, one can refer for example to the P levels for speaking and listening. P4 is:

> Pupils repeat, copy and imitate between 10 and 20 single words, signs or phrases or use a repertoire of objects of reference or symbols. They use single words, signs and symbols for familiar objects, *for example, cup, biscuit*, and to communicate about events and feelings, *for example, likes and dislikes*. They respond appropriately to simple requests which contain one key word, sign or symbol in familiar situations, *for example, Get your coat, Stand up, or Clap your hands*. They show an understanding of familiar objects.
>
> (DfEE 2001, p. 25, italics in original to indicate
> examples particular to speaking and listening)

The description for P8 for speaking and listening is:

> Pupils link up to four key words, signs or symbols in communicating about their own experiences or in telling familiar stories, both in groups and one-to-one, *for example, 'The hairy giant shouted at Finn'*. They use a growing vocabulary to convey meaning to the listener. They take part in role-play with confidence. They listen attentively. They follow requests and instructions with four key words, signs and symbols, *for example, Get the big book about dinosaurs from the library.*
>
> (ibid., p. 25, italics in original)

Profound and multiple learning difficulty

The description of PMLD in the guidance, *Data Collection by Types of Special Educational Needs* states of these pupils, 'Their attainments are likely to remain in the early P scale range (P1–P4) throughout their school careers (that is below level 1 of the National Curriculum) (DfES 2003a, p. 4).

It may be useful to be reminded of examples of these levels. The earlier P level descriptions are generic in that they are the same from P1 to P3 for different subjects such as English, mathematics and science. Each is further subdivided to give P1(i), P1(ii), P2(i), P2(ii), P3(i) and P3(ii). P1(i) is: 'Pupils encounter activities and experiences. They may be passive or resistant. They may show simple reflex responses, *for example, startling at sudden noises or movements*. Any participation is fully prompted' (ibid., p. 36, italics in original).

An example of P4 for speaking and listening was quoted in the previous section. To take a further example, P4 for science is:

> Pupils explore objects and materials provided, changing some materials by physical means and observing the outcomes, *for example when mixing flour and water*. They know that certain actions produce predictable results, *for example, that sponges can be squeezed*. Pupils communicate their awareness of changes in light, sound or movement. They imitate actions involving main body parts, *for example, clapping or stamping*. They make sounds using their own body parts, *for example, tapping, singing or vocalising, and imitate or copy sounds*. They cause movement by a pushing or pulling action. Pupils show interest in a wide range of living things, handling and observing them, *for example, on a visit to a farm, or on a walk in the woods collecting items*.
>
> (ibid., p. 37, italics in original)

When a person is considered to have PMLD, their degree of learning difficulty is such that they are functioning at a developmental level of two years or less. As Ware (2003, p. v) indicates, in practice the developmental level is often well under a year. A child or young person with PMLD may have one or more other severe impairments such as severe visual impairment or very limited mobility and these in turn make learning even more difficult.

Behavioural, emotional and social difficulties and achievement and progress

Behavioural, emotional and social difficulties (BESD) may also be understood in terms of standards of achievement in the broad sense of emotional, behavioural and social development and attitudes to learning. It is not practical to relate behaviour, emotional development and social development to national tests and tasks. Nevertheless, underpinning judgements that a child has BESD is some form of comparison with what is reasonably expected of children of the same age. This may be related to standardised tests of development, the judgements of teachers, parents, psychologists and others informed by their experience of other children. Such judgements are of course somewhat subjective and they are informed by the quality of the teaching and the behaviour management and pastoral approaches of the school and by other factors.

In the particular case of pupils with attention deficit hyperactivity disorder (ADHD), the guidance states that they 'may have reduced attention and impulsivity' (DfES 2003a, p. 4). If these pupils do not have reduced attention and impulsivity, one could fairly ask why the term ADHD is being applied to them at all. From an educational perspective, one can regard such behaviour (that is behaviour giving evidence of reduced attention and impulsivity) as indicating, in developmental or achievement terms, lower levels of attention and lower control of impulsive behaviour than is expected in a child of the same age.

Communication and interaction needs

SPEECH, LANGUAGE AND COMMUNICATION NEEDS

The guidance on types of SEN speaks of pupils with 'speech, language and communication needs', saying that 'Their acquisition of speech and their oral language skills may be significantly behind their peers' (DfES 2003a, p. 5).

AUTISTIC SPECTRUM DISORDER

The guidance on types of SEN indicates that pupils with autistic spectrum disorder (ASD) 'cover the full range of ability and the severity of their impairment varies widely' (DfES 2003a, p. 5). This range of ability however does not apply to the developmental aspects that define ASD, otherwise it would not make sense to speak of any kind of disorder. The guidance states that pupils with ASD find it difficult to 'understand and use verbal communication; understand social behaviour–which affects their ability to interact with adults; think and behave flexibly–which may be shown in restricted, obsessional or repetitive activities' (ibid., p. 5).

Sensory and/or physical needs and attainment and progress

Sensory and/or physical needs refer to hearing impairment, visual impairment, multi-sensory impairment and physical disability. As indicated earlier, attainment and progress do not in part define the impairment or disability. Attainment and progress do however give an indication that the educational provision is appropriate and that it is enabling access to learning and the curriculum. The appropriateness of provision is indicated by what it is considered the pupils 'need' or 'require' as the sub-sections below illustrate.

VISUAL IMPAIRMENT

The guidance on types of SEN indicates that pupils with visual impairment 'require adaptations to their environment or specific differentiation of learning materials in order to access the curriculum' (DfES 2003a, p. 6). This 'requirement' is related to the degree of visual impairment experienced.

HEARING IMPAIRMENT

The guidance indicates that pupils with hearing impairment, 'require hearing aids, adaptations to their environment and/or particular teaching strategies in order to access the concepts of language and the curriculum' (DfES 2003a, p. 6). The 'requirement' is again related to the degree of impairment, in this case hearing impairment.

MULTI-SENSORY IMPAIRMENT

The document *Data Collection by Type of Special Educational Need* indicates what it considers to be the 'needs' of pupils with multi-sensory impairment (that is pupils who have a combination of visual and hearing impairments). These pupils, 'need teaching approaches which make good use of their residual hearing and vision, together with their other senses.' They may also 'need alternative means of communication' (DfES 2003a, p. 7).

PHYSICAL

The guidance applies to pupils who have a physical disability that gives rise to a SEN. It states that 'Some pupils are mobile but have significant fine motor difficulties which require support. Others may need augmentative or alternative communication aids' (DfES 2003a, p. 7).

OTHER SEN

The category of 'other SEN' is intended for 'very unusual special educational needs which are substantially different from those described' (DfES 2003, p. 7).

Local criteria/thresholds for SEN

If special education is understood as a moral response involving preferential provision to pupils with SEN, additional to or different from that of other pupils, it is important that SEN is clearly defined. Well-understood local criteria for SEN are part of this approach. This is not without its challenges. For example, there is a tension between attempts by LEAs to establish criteria for SEN and the individual approach to cases in appeals to the Special Educational Needs and Disability Tribunal (Farrell 2004, pp. 17–31).

Among LEA criteria for SEN are those developed by Croydon LEA (Farrell 2004a, pp. 23–4), Northamptonshire LEA (ibid., p. 24) and Blackpool LEA (Farrell 2004b, Chapter 2). A group of five London LEAs have also developed criteria which they refer to as 'thresholds': the London Borough of Dagenham, the London Borough of Bexley, The Learning Trust (for Hackney LEA), the London Borough of Haringey and the London Borough of Greenwich (London SEN Regional Partnership 2004 and www.londonsen.org.uk). Other LEAs, working with the West Midlands SEN Regional Partnership, are also developing joint criteria: Birmingham, Coventry, Dudley, Herefordshire, Sandwell, Shropshire, Solihull, Staffordshire, Stoke-on-Trent, Telford and Wrekin, Walsall, Warwickshire, Wolverhampton and Worcestershire.

Case study 1: LEA criteria for the statutory assessment of SEN

This case study considers the criteria used by Bracknell Forest LEA, in relation to the statutory assessment of SEN. It draws from the 2002 document *Bracknell Forest Borough Council Revised Criteria for Carrying Out Statutory Assessments of Special Educational Needs, Drawing Up Statements of Special Educational Needs and Ceasing Statements of Special Educational Needs* (hereafter the *Revised Criteria*). Bracknell Forest recognises that, when deciding whether or not to proceed to a statutory assessment or issue a statement of SEN, any determination of a child's lower attainments indicated by norm-referenced tests forms part of the picture. It has to be considered with judgements on whether the child is making adequate progress in the light of what has been provided by the school and others.

The *Revised Criteria* outlines the national framework for SEN, the legal basis and the LEA's policy. It explains the *Special Educational Needs Code of Practice* (DfES 2001) graduated response. The *Revised Criteria* sets out the criteria for deciding to make a statutory assessment, the approach for children under five, criteria for deciding to draft a statement and the procedures for ceasing a statement of SEN.

This case study concerns the criteria that the LEA has for deciding to make a statutory assessment. These are made available to all professionals working with children with SEN in the authority. The authority operates a moderating group to consider individual cases according to criteria for statutory assessment and the issuing of a statement and the group includes educational psychologist and head teacher representation. The *Revised Criteria* covers communication and interaction difficulties including autistic spectrum disorder; cognition and learning difficulties; specific learning difficulties; behavioural, emotional and social difficulties; sensory difficulties (hearing impairment and visual impairment), physical difficulties; and medical conditions (to the extent that they may sometimes lead to special educational needs).

Key evidence

Among the key evidence that the LEA considers when deciding whether a statutory assessment might be necessary is that relating to academic attainment understood in the context of:

- the attainments of the child's peers – the *comparative* element
- the child's progress over time – the *progressive* element
- (where appropriate) expectations of the child's performance – the *predictive* element.

The LEA will be alert to:

- significant discrepancies between the child's attainments in assessments and tests in the core subjects of the National Curriculum against the attainment of the majority of children of his or her own age – as indicated by the table below
- significant discrepancies between the child's attainments in assessments and tests in the core subjects of the National Curriculum against the performance expected of the child as indicated by a consensus of those who have taught and observed the child, including the parents and supported by such standardised tests as can be reliably administered
- significant discrepancies between a child's attainment within one core subject or across different core subjects of the National Curriculum.

Table 2.1 National Curriculum levels of attainment

	Key Stage 1	*Key Stage 2*	*Key Stage 3*
Target levels for schemes of work for the great majority *	Levels 1 to 3	Levels 2 to 5	Levels 3 to 7
Performance significantly below majority at the end of the Key Stage #	Working towards Level 1	Working within or below Level 2	Working within or below Level 3

* As set out in the statutory National Curriculum Orders
\# As derived from national end of key stage assessment data

The examples of the *Revised Guidance* criteria chosen for this case study are: cognition and learning difficulties; specific learning difficulties, and autistic spectrum disorder.

Cognition and learning

Criteria for deciding to assess

Where a child has moderate, severe or profound and multiple learning needs:

- the general level of attainment will be significantly below that of peers, as identified through National Curriculum levels of attainment and reliably administered standardised tests
- there will be difficulty in acquiring basic literacy and numeracy skills
- in many cases there will be significant speech and language difficulties
- in some cases there will be immature motor development
- in some cases there will be poor social skills
- some may show persistent signs of emotional and behavioural difficulties.

There will be evidence that a child with cognition and learning difficulties may require some or all of the following:

- flexible teaching arrangements
- help with processing language, memory and reasoning skills
- help and support in acquiring literacy skills
- help in organising and co-ordinating spoken and written English to aid cognition
- help with sequencing and organisational skills
- programmes to aid improvement of fine or gross motor skills
- support in the use of technical terms and abstract ideas
- help in understanding ideas, concepts and experiences when information cannot be gained through first-hand sensory or physical experiences.

Children in the following age groups will demonstrate deficits in development of basic skill attainment of at least the order of magnitude shown in the table on the next two pages.

Table 2.2 Chronological age and assessment or screening outcomes

Chronological age	Assessment or screening outcomes
Reception	– Surrey Screening Profile/baseline assessment predominantly at the 1st percentile – ability or development profiles at or below the 3-year level, for example in cognitive, language and self-help skills – standardised scores of below 70 on a reading/literacy test administered by an educational psychologist
Year 1	– no measurable attainment on literacy and numeracy scales standardised for Key Stage 1 – ability or development profiles below the 4-year level, particularly in cognitive, language and self-help areas – standardised scores of below 70 on a reading/literacy test administered by an educational psychologist
Year 2 National Curriculum core subjects: working towards L1	– quotients or standardised scores below 70 on language, literacy or numeracy tests administered by an educational psychologist – quotients or standardised scores below 70 on school-based standardised screening tests of reading and number
Year 3 National Curriculum core subjects: mostly working towards L1	– standardised scores at basal limit on WORD* – quotients or standardised scores below 70 on school-based standardised screening tests of reading and number development
Year 4 National Curriculum core subjects: some attainments at L1	– reading and spelling standardised scores below 6-year equivalent on WORD* quotients or standardised scores below 70 on school-based standardised screening tests of reading and number development
Year 5 National Curriculum core subjects: attainments at L1 and working within L2	– reading and spelling standardised scores at or below 6-year equivalent on WORD* quotients or standardised scores below 70 on school-based standardised screening tests of reading and number

Continued

Chronological age	Assessment or screening outcomes
Year 6 National Curriculum core subjects: LI generally attained and working towards L2	– reading and spelling standardised scores at or below 6½-year equivalent on WORD* – quotients or standardised scores below 70 on school-based standardised screening tests of reading and number
Year 7 National Curriculum core subjects: mostly working towards L2	– reading and spelling standardised scores at or below 6½-year equivalent on WORD* – quotients or standardised scores below 70 on school-based standardised screening tests of reading and number

*   closed test

Other factors

In deciding whether to carry out a statutory assessment, the LEA will also ask whether:

- the child is not benefiting from work on National Curriculum Programmes of Study relevant to his/her key stage or has been formally disapplied from National Curriculum requirements
- there is evidence that the child is falling progressively behind the majority of children of his/her age, taking into consideration the child's assessed levels of cognitive ability or functioning, for example an assessment of attainment showing a child moving from the 5th percentile to the 2nd percentile. However, the LEA will not carry out a statutory assessment solely because the child is falling progressively behind others: there would need to be evidence of the extent of the disparity over time and of the child's cognitive ability
- there is evidence of a significant discrepancy between the child's assessed levels of mechanical reading, for example on a word recognition test or a test assessing the ability to read a complete sentence, and his or her assessed levels of comprehension, for example on a sentence completion test or other test addressing comprehension

- there is evidence of inadequate personal independence or organisation, or impaired social interaction or communication, or a significantly restricted repertoire of activities, interests and imaginative development
- there is evidence of significant emotional or behavioural difficulties that are directly affecting the capacity of the child to learn in the classroom
- there is evidence of contributory or remediable medical problems – this will be of particular importance in the case of children with severe or profound and multiple learning difficulties.

Cognition and learning needs – the special educational provision already made

In deciding whether to carry out a statutory assessment, the LEA will consider the action taken by the school and, in particular, whether the actions set out in the LEA checklist have been carried out. (This checklist is part of the Revised Criteria document.)

Cognition and learning needs – summary criteria for a statutory assessment

The LEA will carry out a statutory assessment where the balance of evidence assessed against the above criteria suggests that the child's learning difficulties:

- are significant and/or complex
- remain or have not been remedied sufficiently, despite the school, with the help of external specialists, having taken relevant and purposeful action to meet the learning difficulties
- may require the LEA to determine the child's special educational provision – particularly if this calls for special educational provision which cannot reasonably be provided within the resources normally available to mainstream maintained schools and settings in the area.

Specific learning difficulties

Additional considerations

Where a child has specific learning difficulties, in addition to the considerations set out earlier under 'key evidence':

- there may be significant difficulties in reading, writing, spelling, or manipulating numbers, which are not typical of the child's general levels of performance
- he or she may gain some skills in some subjects quickly and demonstrate a high level of ability orally, yet may encounter sustained difficulty in gaining literacy or numeracy skills
- there may be severe frustration and emotional or behavioural difficulties.

Specific learning difficulties and levels of attainment in literacy

In determining whether the child's levels of attainment in literacy are significantly below that of his peers, and whether in consequence a statutory assessment is needed, the LEA will require good evidence of attainments in reading falling so far outside the expected range that no more than one child in every hundred would attain similarly as shown in Table 2.3 on the following page.

Mathematics and spelling are not regarded as access skills in the same way as reading. Development in these areas will be considered alongside significant difficulties in acquiring reading skills. The LEA will not carry out a statutory assessment solely on the grounds that there are significant difficulties in mathematics or spelling.

Other factors

In deciding whether to carry out a statutory assessment, the LEA will seek clear, recorded evidence of the child's academic attainment and ask, for example, whether:

Table 2.3 *Chronological age and scores on a test of reading*

Chronological age	Test of basic reading (WORD*)
7 years 0 months	N/A
8 years 0 months	basal limit of test (raw score zero)
8 years 6 months	< 6 years (raw score 2 or fewer)
9 years 0 months	< 6 years
9 years 6 months	6 years 0 months (raw score 8 or fewer)
10 years 0 months	6 years 0 months
10 years 6 months	6 years 3 months
11 years 0 months	6 years 3 months
11 years 6 months	6 years 3 months
12 years 0 months	6 years 6 months
12 years 6 months	6 years 6 months
13 years 0 months	6 years 9 months
13 years 6 months	7 years 0 months
14 years 0 months	7 years 3 months

* closed test

- there are extreme discrepancies between attainments in different core subjects of the National Curriculum, or within one core subject, especially where attainment in *Speaking and Listening* is significantly higher than in reading or writing
- expectations of the child, as indicated by a consensus of those who have taught or observed the child, supported as appropriate by reliably administered tests of cognitive ability or oral comprehension, are significantly above his or her attainments in National Curriculum assessments and tests and/or the results of reliably administered standardised reading, spelling or mathematics tests. In reviewing such evidence,
- the LEA will look for evidence that the child is close to meeting the criteria in relation to 'key evidence' and *either* there has been no significant progress over an extended period *or* the statistical probability of such discrepancy would be found in fewer than one child in a hundred
- the LEA will consider a reading age equivalent to the 9½ level to be the level of competence which should give access to most

relevant curriculum materials. Attainment of this level would be a basis from which progress should be made, without needing additional support outside the resources available to mainstream schools

• there is evidence of clumsiness, significant difficulties in sequencing or visual perception, deficiencies in working memory or significant delays in language functioning as indicated by a consensus of professionals who know the child or reliably administered standardised tests (which are now available for all such areas of potential difficulty).

The Language and Literacy Centre

The Language and Literacy Centre offers programmes devised and overseen by specialist teachers, usually arranged by attendance once a week at the Centre. Pupils in Key Stage 2 who are assessed as having severe or complex specific learning difficulties should usually be referred for intervention through the Language and Literacy Centre before consideration is given to a statutory assessment. Only if special circumstances in a particular case make such referral inappropriate or a place cannot be offered within a reasonable length of time, will consideration be given to moving to statutory assessment without such an intervention having taken place.

Autistic spectrum disorder

In addition to the considerations relating to communication and interaction (these are set out in the *Revised Criteria* document) there are a number of additional considerations when a child has social communication difficulties that may lie on the autistic spectrum.

The autistic spectrum describes a pervasive developmental disorder, associated with impairment in social awareness, social communication and imagination. One end of the spectrum is frequently associated with severe learning difficulties, and, sometimes, challenging or very withdrawn behaviour. At the other end of the spectrum, many of the child's cognitive difficulties will lie within the normal range, and the child's social impairment will be more subtle, evident only through longer-term assessment and observation.

In the case of autistic spectrum disorder, early recognition, possibly with diagnosis, and specialist support are essential to facilitate the critical development of social and communication skills. Although diagnosis through specialist assessment within the NHS Trust will be helpful, diagnosis in itself is not a prerequisite for consideration of the child's SEN by the LEA. Nor will the LEA expect to carry out a statutory assessment *solely* because there is a diagnosis of an autistic spectrum condition.

Children with severe autism are more likely to be identified as having SEN in their early years, whereas the needs of children with, for example, Asperger's Syndrome or high functioning autism, have often been identified much later, during Key Stages 1 or 2.

Autistic spectrum disorder – the child's learning difficulty

Children with severe autism will have a combination of difficulties. They may have needs associated with communication and interaction, cognition and learning, behaviour, emotional and social development.

Consideration should be given to presentation of evidence in relation to any of these aspects. The LEA will always seek evidence of the child's academic attainment and speech and language development (with advice from a speech and language therapist) as well as the nature and extent of the *triad of difficulties*: social communication, social awareness, and imagination.

In all cases, when deciding whether to carry out a statutory assessment, the LEA will ask, for example, whether:

• the child is not benefiting from work on National Curriculum Programmes of Study relevant to his/her key stage or has been formally disapplied from National Curriculum requirements
• there is evidence of inadequate personal independence or organisation, or impaired social interaction, reciprocity or

communication, or a significantly restricted repertoire of activities, interests and imaginative development
- there is clear, substantiated evidence, based on specific examples, that the child's social communication difficulties impede the development of purposeful relationships appropriate to his/her developmental level with adults and/or peers across a variety of contexts and how this is affected by the social demands of the educational situation in particular
- there is clear evidence, over time, of marked impairment in the use of multiple non-verbal behaviours, such as eye-to-eye gaze, facial expression, body postures and gestures to regulate social interaction
- the child displays challenging, bizarre, obsessive or very withdrawn behaviour, observed and recorded over a period of time
- there is clear evidence, over time, of restricted, repetitive and stereotyped patterns of behaviours, interests and activities, including one or more of the following:

  - encompassing preoccupation with one or more stereotyped and restricted patterns of interest that is abnormal in intensity or focus
  - apparently inflexible adherence to specific, non-functional routines
  - stereotyped and repetitive movement mannerisms, e.g. hand or finger flapping or twisting or complex whole-body movements
  - persistent preoccupation with parts of objects
  - there is clear evidence of a consistent lack of spontaneous seeking to share enjoyment, interests or achievements with other people
  - there is evidence that provides an analysis of the child's play and preferences during unstructured periods of the day.

(from *Revised Criteria* with the kind permission of Bracknell Forest LEA)

Summary/conclusion

This chapter examined the definitions of types of SEN provided in the Pupil Level Annual School Census (PLASC) guidance (DfES 2003a) in relation to pupils' attainment and progress.

I maintained that criteria are necessary to refine definitions of SEN and looked at how these relate to standards of pupil attainment and progress. A case study illustrated LEA thresholds/criteria for the statutory assessment of certain types of SEN.

Thinking points

Readers may wish to consider:

- the practicalities of developing agreement on criteria for types of SEN and how they could contribute to the process
- examining in detail the criteria developed by LEAs such as those mentioned earlier
- the possibility of working with other LEAs (perhaps through a SEN Regional Partnership) to agree criteria across a group of LEAs.

Key texts

Department for Education and Skills (2003a) *Data Collecting by Type of Special Educational Needs,* London, DfES

This document provides brief definitions of different categories of SEN to assist the LEA in completing their Pupil Level Annual School Census (PLASC) returns.

Farrell, M. (2004a) *Special Educational Needs: A Resource for Practitioners,* London, Paul Chapman Publishing

Chapter 3 relates the legal definition of SEN to local criteria. It provides case studies of criteria for initiating the statutory assessment of SEN developed by Croydon LEA (pp. 23–4) and criteria for the involvement of qualified teachers of the visually impaired and of qualified teachers of the deaf (p. 24) developed by Northamptonshire LEA.

How identifying, assessing and providing for pupils with **SEN** is informed by pupils' standards and progress

Introduction

This chapter examines the *Special Educational Needs Code of Practice* (Department for Education and Skills 2001a) hereafter in this chapter referred to as the *Code,* with particular reference to pupils' attainment, achievement and progress and to providing pupils access to learning and the curriculum.

I then outline the main components of approaches to guidance on identification and assessment (and to a lesser degree provision) as they relate to requests for statutory assessment. A case study illustrates the approach of a group of LEAs to guidance on requests for the statutory assessment of pupils with SEN.

The previous chapters considered the legal definition of SEN (Chapter 1) and definitions of types of SEN (Chapter 2). Relationships between such definitions and the identification and assessment of SEN should be apparent. If one is to identify pupils considered to have SEN, it is necessary to be clear what SEN and types of SEN are considered to be. Similarly, if one is to assess pupils considered to have SEN, it is necessary to know whom and what is being assessed. Provision follows such identification and assessment.

The *Special Educational Needs Code of Practice*

The **Code**: *Tension between 'meeting needs' and encouraging achievement and progress*

Following an earlier version introduced in 1994, a revised *Code,* published in 2001, came into effect in January 2002. It provides advice for local education authorities (LEAs), maintained schools, early education settings and others on their responsibilities towards all children with SEN. The *Code* takes account of the SEN provisions of the *Special Educational Needs and Disability Act 2001* expressed as various rights and duties. These are:

- a stronger right for children with SEN to be educated at a mainstream school
- new duties on LEAs to arrange for the parents of children with SEN to be provided with services offering advice and information and a means of resolving disputes
- a new duty requiring schools and relevant nursery education providers to tell parents when they make special educational provision for their child
- a new right for schools and relevant nursery education providers to request a statutory assessment for a child.
    (Department for Education and Skills 2001a, Foreword, paragraph 7)

The *Code* recommends that, in order to help match special educational provision to children's needs, schools and LEAs adopt a graduated approach. An aspect of this in early education settings and schools is, respectively, 'Early Years Action' and 'School Action'. Where outside advice and intervention is required, the graduated approach involves 'Early Years Action Plus' and 'School Action Plus'. It is expected that a minority of children with the most severe and complex SEN will undergo a statutory assessment that may lead to a statement of SEN being agreed.

The document seeks to provide practical guidance to various parties on the discharge of their functions under part 4 of the Education Act 1996. The parties concerned are:

- local education authorities (LEAs)
- the governing bodies of all maintained schools and settings in receipt of government funding to provide early education, and
- those who help the above (including health services and social services).
    (Department for Education and Skills 2001a, Chapter 1, section 1)

The *Code* (1.2) sets out guidance on policies and procedures that aim to enable pupils with SEN to reach their full potential, be fully included in their school communities, and make a successful transition to adulthood. It is permeated with references to pupils' standards of attainment, their standards of achievement, their progress and references to improving access to learning and the curriculum. More vaguely, it often refers to 'needs' and 'meeting needs'.

One of the fundamental principles of the *Code* is that children with SEN 'should have their needs met' (1.5). A critical success factor is that 'the culture, practice, management and deployment of resources in a school or setting are designed to ensure **all children's needs are met**' (1.6, bold in original). The *Code* advises that a range of strategies are adopted that recognise 'the various complexities of need, the different responsibilities to assess and meet those needs, and the associated range and variations in provision, which will best reflect and promote common recognition of the continuum of special educational needs' (1.37).

Difficulties with the word 'need' have been recognised by many. For example, deciding children's 'needs' is far from approaching an objective process and in determining needs it is necessary to establish what is required for a particular end (Farrell 2003b, p. 110). Accordingly, a distinction can be made between 'goal-directed needs' (I need food in order to survive) and 'unconditional need' (that is, supposed needs for which the goal is not specified; this pupil 'needs' ten hours of support time from a learning support assistant) (Farrell 2004b, Chapter 2, Passim). In practice if it is remembered that attainment, achievement and progress inform the definition of special educational need, the use of the term can be more meaningful.

Nevertheless, the *Code* is at its vaguest when it speaks of 'needs' and 'meeting needs' without specifying what the supposed needs are, why they are considered to be needs and how anyone would know if and when those needs were met. For example, Chapter 2 of the *Code* concerns 'Working in partnership with parents' and speaks of children's 'needs' without reference to standards of pupil achievement.

However, when addressing 'Pupil participation' (Chapter 3), the *Code* states, in referring to Individual Education Plans (IEPs), that, 'If children are involved in the IEP process, then *achievements* can be noted and celebrated as well as any difficulties clarified and addressed' (3.11, italics added). Suggesting that young people with SEN may have low self-esteem and lack self confidence, the chapter states that:

> Actively encouraging these pupils to track their own *progress* and record *achievement* within a programme of action designed to meet their particular learning or behavioural difficulty will contribute to improved confidence and self image.

> (3.14, italics added)

The implied empowerment aspect of self image (and self-esteem) is reflected in the way self-esteem is understood. For example, one set of materials to assess and develop self-esteem (and which are considered in more detail in the present text in Chapter 5) conceptualise self-esteem as involving three components: sense of self, sense of belonging, and sense of personal power (Morris 2002c, p. 5, secondary materials).

Identification, assessment and provision in the Code

Most of the references in the *Code* to attainment, achievement, progress and gaining access to learning and the curriculum (where attainment, achievement and progress are indicators that such access is gained) are unsurprisingly in the chapters directly concerning identification, assessment and provision. These are Chapters 4–7.

Chapter 4 concerns 'Identification, assessment and provision in early education settings'. The Government's 'Early Learning Goals' set out what most children will achieve in various 'areas' (e.g. communication) by the time they enter year 1 of primary education. Early education (for children aged three to five years) is known as the 'foundation stage' of education. The identification of SEN is related to slow progress in the foundation stage. The provider intervenes through 'Early Years Action' and, if progress is still not satisfactory, the SEN co-ordinator may seek advice and support from external agencies ('Early Years Action Plus') (Department for Education and Skills, 2001a, 4.11–4.13).

Various 'triggers' are proposed to indicate that intervention could be necessary at 'Early Years Action' (4.21). A (progress) trigger is that the child 'makes little or no progress even when teaching approaches are particularly targeted to improve the child's identified area of weakness'. Another progress trigger is that the child 'has sensory or physical problems, and continues to make little or no progress despite the provision of personal aids and equipment'. A standards trigger is that the child 'continues working at levels significantly below those expected for children of a similar age in certain areas' (4.21).

Triggers are also indicated for outside intervention through Early Years Action Plus. These also concern standards, progress and access. One (standards) trigger is that the child 'continues working at an early years curriculum substantially below that expected of children of a similar age' (4.31). Another (progress) trigger is that the child 'continues to make little or no progress in specific areas over a long period' (4.31). A further (progress) trigger that is expressed in terms of access is that the child has 'ongoing communication or interaction difficulties that impede the development of social relationships and cause substantial barriers to learning' (4.31). In this last situation, the difficulties 'impede development' so that progress in the development of social relationships presumably is not satisfactory in terms of the *Code,* and learning is hindered.

Chapter 5 of the *Code* deals with 'Identification, assessment and provision in the primary phase' (five to 11 years or National Curriculum years 1 to 6) and provides guidance on 'School Action' and 'School Action Plus'. Triggers for School Action deal with progress and attainment. One progress trigger, for example, concerns sensory or physical problems and the child 'continues to make little or no progress despite the provision of specialist equipment' (5.44). An attainment trigger is that the child 'shows signs of difficulty in developing literacy or mathematics skills which result in poor attainment in some curriculum areas' (5.44). Another trigger that implies unsatisfactory progress and perhaps relates to access to learning is that the child 'presents persistent emotional or behavioural difficulties which are not ameliorated by the behaviour management techniques usually employed in the school' (5.44).

Triggers for School Action Plus involve standards of attainment, progress and access. Each trigger assumes that the child has already been receiving an individualised programme and/or concentrated support under School Action. One (progress) trigger is that the child still 'continues to make little or no progress in specific areas over a long period' (5.56). Another (standards) trigger is that the child 'continues working at National Curriculum levels considerably below that expected of children of a similar age' (5.56). A target relating to progress and access is that the child 'has ongoing communication or interaction difficulties that impede the development of social relationships and cause substantial barriers to learning' (5.56).

Chapter 6 covers 'Identification, assessment and provision in the secondary sector' giving guidance on 'School Action' and 'School Action Plus'. Triggers for School Action involve progress, attainment and (possibly) access. A progress trigger is that the child or young person 'has sensory or physical problems, and continues to make little or no progress despite the provision of specialist equipment' (6.51). An attainment trigger is that the pupil 'shows signs of difficulty in developing literacy or mathematics skills that result in poor attainment in some curriculum areas' (6.51). A trigger that appears to include progress and access is that the pupil, 'presents persistent emotional and/or behavioural difficulties, which are not ameliorated by the behaviour management techniques usually employed in the school' (6.51).

School Action Plus triggers again deal with standards of attainment and access. A progress trigger is that the pupil 'continues to have difficulty in developing literacy and mathematics skills' (6.64). An attainment trigger is that the pupil 'continues working at National Curriculum levels substantially below that expected of pupils of a similar age' (6.64). A trigger relating to access to learning (of both the pupil with SEN and other pupils) is that the pupil 'has emotional or behavioural difficulties which substantially and regularly interfere with their own learning or that of the class group, despite having an individualised behaviour management programme' (6.64).

Chapter 7, 'Statutory assessment of SEN', has to do with the duties of a LEA under the Education Act 1996 sections 321 and 323 to identify and make a statutory assessment of those children for whom they are responsible who have SEN and who probably need a statement. In considering a request for the statutory assessment of a pupil, the LEA 'will always require evidence of the child's academic attainment in all areas of learning' (7.38). Also, '… attainment is the essential starting point when considering the evidence' (7.40). Among the questions the LEA might ask is whether 'there is evidence that the child is falling *progressively* behind the majority of children of their age in academic attainment in any of the National Curriculum core subjects … ' (7.41 italics added).

General features for identification and assessment in relation to requests for statutory assessment

Clear procedures and communication

Whatever the local arrangements for identification, assessment of pupils with SEN in relation to requests for statutory assessment, roles, timing and communications need to be clear. There should be guidance as to who determines whether to start the statutory assessment process and how they come to this decision. Similarly, it should be clear who will record the decision whether or not to carry out a statutory assessment and how this is conveyed to the school or/and parent concerned.

What has been done already?

In deciding whether to initiate a statutory assessment, the LEA will require that the school has procedures in place and has tried suitable interventions already. It will request evidence of this to make a well-informed judgement.

The school SEN policy will indicate whether the school has broad approaches to support pupils with SEN. Depending on the type of SEN, other policies, such as those for behaviour, language development, pastoral support, will be important. These are likely to indicate how the school directs resources to pupils with SEN and how the ethos of the school contributes. Evidence for this could be in the policies themselves and an evaluation of their impact.

Parents will have been kept informed and the school will have worked closely with them. Indications of this will be in notes of meetings, other records of contact with parents and the outcomes.

There will have been successive assessments to monitor the pupil's progress, and interventions, such as allocating extra teaching time, will have been tried. Individual Education Plans (IEP) will outline the interventions and their impact over a specified period, perhaps of six months. Before statutory assessment is considered, there will normally have been interventions at the School Action Plus or Early Years Action Plus part of the graduated response. This will have involved support from services external to the school. Evidence of this might be recorded in the advice provided and the interventions implemented.

Other individual differences may have been taken into account in assessing SEN and in monitoring progress. These include the gender of the pupil, whether English is spoken as an additional language, social background, cultural background, age and other factors (see Chapter 8). Indications of this will be in the schools' analyses of such data.

What is the situation now?

In determining whether a statutory assessment is required, the LEA will need to know the pupil's present situation.

The school will know the attainments of the pupil and the progress that has already been made. It will have observed behaviour and the responses of the pupil as appropriate. This may be indicated, for example, by the results of National Curriculum tests and tasks, standardised and other assessments, observation schedules (for example of the pupil's behaviour), pupil self-assessments (perhaps of self-esteem) and so on. Some of these may be drawn from school reports and collated. Data on progress may be informed by target-setting in comparison with other schools to provide benchmarked information that gives an indication of 'value added' (see Chapters 4 and 5). Reports from specialists external to the school will also give evidence of standards of attainment and progress.

What is proposed for the future?

Drawing on the past progress and the present attainment of the pupil, the school can indicate what provision it considers will benefit the pupil if assessment leads to extra funding and support in the form of a statement. This provision or intervention may be specified in terms of the curriculum; teaching and assessment and other aspects of school organisation; staffing; accommodation; resources and external support.

In relation to the curriculum, the school may propose to modify the pupil's curriculum to emphasise an aspect that would be likely to benefit the child. For example, for a pupil with language and communication difficulties, emphasis could be placed on speaking and listening, alternative or augmented communication, or group discussion. For a pupil with behavioural, emotional and social difficulties, the cathartic aspects of certain subjects such as art, drama, physical education and music might be highlighted, or specific therapies might be built into the curriculum including art, music and drama therapy. Opportunities for mobility training or social communication are among other curricular modifications that might be proposed for other pupils.

Teaching and assessment, and the support of other staff might also be indicated. For example, the pupil might be considered to benefit from specialist teaching or from individual or group counselling.

School organisation involves the grouping of pupils in sets, streams and other forms of whole school groupings as well as setting up (perhaps within a class) provision for work in small groups, pairs and individual support.

Modifications to the school accommodation or its use of accommodation might be proposed. This might simply be ensuring that there is a quiet space for individual or small groupwork with the pupil. Particular resources over and above what the school would normally provide might be indicated, such as specialist equipment to support communication or personal hygiene.

A programme of specialist external support might be proposed, perhaps at a more sustained and intensive level than has been possible at the Early Years Action Plus or School Action Plus part of the graduated response.

With reference to the above possible proposals, the main point is that the school in consultation with others has identified:

• what it considers necessary that is not being presently provided, and
• what is required to put the necessary procedures and interventions into place.

There is a coherent, understandable line of graduated response from the past through to the present, and on to proposals for the future.

Case study 2: LEA procedures relating to requests for statutory assessment

Four London LEAs and a Learning Trust have worked together to produce joint guidance relating to requests for statutory assessment and have also developed related criteria (thresholds) (London Special Educational Needs Partnership 2003 and www.londonsen.org.uk). The five bodies are the London Borough of Barking and Dagenham, the London Borough of Bexley, The Learning Trust (for Hackney Local Education Authority), the London Borough of Haringey, and the London Borough of Greenwich. This case study describes some points of the guidance relating to requests for statutory assessment. The joint guidance deals with the present, past and future.

The present is considered through SCAN (the Significance of the Child's Achievements Now). This relates to what the child can do; that is, his or her achievements at the present and the severity, duration and extent of any behaviour difficulties. Information to support any request for statutory assessment may include National Curriculum levels or the results of standardised tests.

For these SCAN elements, thresholds are indicated for Early Years Action/School Action, Early Years Action Plus/School Action Plus, and requests for statutory assessment. These are what I have elsewhere called 'criteria' (see Chapter 2, 'How types of SEN and LEA criteria relate to pupils' standards and progress').

The past is considered using an AUDIT (Assessments Undertaken and Direct Intervention over Time). This explains the extent and quality of what has already been done, for example, what interventions have already been tried and evaluated. Supporting information may include evidence of interventions and their outcome. The AUDIT is considered in relation to LEA arrangements for provision.

The future is considered through a PLAN (Provision Likely to be needed Additional to that Normally available). This is an outline of what is required for future provision. Information to support this may include a programme and information about how it will be delivered and by whom.

Guidance on the SCAN, AUDIT and PLAN requirements and 'general guidance on a graduated response' (thresholds) are provided for different types of SEN as follows:

- Communication and interaction

    - speech and language delay, impairments or disorders
    - disorders on the autistic continuum.

- Cognition and learning

    - Mild, moderate, severe or profound learning difficulty

- Behavioural, emotional, and social difficulties

    - Emotional and behavioural difficulties

- Sensory and/or physical needs

    - Hearing impairment
    - Visual impairment
    - Physical disabilities

- Medical conditions

    - Medical conditions giving rise to SEN

The five LEAs worked together to produce the guidance while each retained its own documented decision-making process including information about how and by whom decisions regarding the commencement of statutory assessment are made, and how and by whom decisions are recorded. It is proposed to review the guidance periodically.

(From information kindly supplied by the London SEN Regional Partnership)

Summary/conclusion

This chapter highlighted the importance of pupils' attainment, achievement and progress in the *Special Educational Needs Code of Practice*. I outlined the main components of approaches to guidance on identification and assessment (and to a lesser degree, provision) relating to requests for statutory assessment. The case study illustrated the approach of four London LEAs and a Learning Trust to guidance on requests for the statutory assessment of a pupil with SEN.

Thinking points

Readers may wish to consider:

* the importance of developing and refining procedures for identifying and assessing pupils with SEN and their own possible contribution to this process
* the relevance of linking identification and assessment with criteria for types of SEN
* the value of LEAs working together to develop joint approaches to identification and assessment
* the eventual prospect of a nationwide agreement on criteria for types of SEN, identification and assessment that might smooth out some of the idiosyncrasies and vagaries of particular LEAs.

Key texts

Department for Education and Skills (2001) *Special Educational Needs Code of Practice,* London: DfES

Readers may wish to reflect on the tension in the document between, on the one hand, the vagueness of meeting 'needs', and on the other hand the potential clarity of improving pupils' attainment, achievement and progress, and improving pupils' access to learning and the curriculum.

Chapter 4

Curriculum and assessment and target-setting in 'academic' areas

Introduction

This chapter outlines the development of the National Curriculum and national assessment in England. I consider curriculum issues and SEN and assessment and SEN, in particular 'accommodations' (that is, allowing flexibility to accommodate the particular requirements of the pupil) and alternative assessments.

The chapter then looks at matters arising for target-setting, in particular potentially negative effects of target-setting on schools working with pupils with SEN, and statutory targets as a possible inhibitor of mainstream inclusion. I then explain procedures for target-setting with pupils having SEN with the example of literacy targets.

Finally, the chapter touches on the approaches of benchmarking and value-added measures for pupils with SEN. A case study illustrates the use of P scales for improving pupils' writing skills in a special school.

The National Curriculum and national assessment

In England and Wales, the Conservative government voted into power in 1979 introduced the Education Reform Act 1998 with a view to raising educational standards. The Act shifted responsibility for the content of the curriculum and its delivery, and for assessment from local education authorities, schools and teachers towards to central government. This involved provision for:

- a national curriculum
- a national system of assessment and testing at ages seven, 11, 14 and 16
- open enrolment

- competition between schools for pupil places
- parental preferences for schools
- the setting up of other types of schools outside local education authority control
- more financial independence for schools through such developments as local management for schools and local management for special schools.

School provision was seen in key stages. Key Stage 1 was for pupils in year groups 1 and 2 (ages five through seven years). Key Stage 2 referred to years 3 through 6 (ages seven through 11 years). Key Stage 3 was for pupils in years 7 through 9 (ages 11 through 14 years). Key Stage 4 related to pupils in years 10 and 11 (ages 15 to 16 years). National Curriculum subjects were English, mathematics and science (the 'core' subjects) and the 'foundation' subjects of technology, geography, history, physical education, art, music and (for Key Stage 3) a modern foreign language.

Programmes of study specified what should be taught, and expected standards of pupil attainment were set out in 'attainment targets'. In 1995, the National Curriculum was reviewed and 'level descriptions' were introduced for most subjects, although for art, music and physical education, 'key stage descriptions' were used instead. The level descriptions allowed teachers to give indications of pupils' levels of attainment. At the end of each key stage, summative assessments were introduced involving teacher assessment and 'external' tests and tasks (also known as Standards Assessment Tests/Tasks or SATs).

At the end of Key Stage 4, pupil achievement is predominantly assessed through pupil examinations such as the General Certificate of Secondary Education (GCSE) and the General National Vocational Qualifications (GNVQs) in various subjects. Present day alternative accreditation includes the Award Scheme Development and Accreditation Network (ASDAN) (www.asdan.co.uk) and Entry Level Certificates such as those offered by the Welsh Joint Education Committee (www.wjec.co.uk).

A review of the National Curriculum led to various changes, including the provision of 'access statements' in each subject order. These encourage:

- the use of aids
- adaptations to equipment
- adaptations to communication

- work on curriculum content to help ensure its relevance to pupils with SEN
- a more important place for personal and social education.

In a further revision of the National Curriculum for 2000, more changes were made, including greater attention to personal and social education and the addition of a statement of inclusion. This inclusion statement sets out three principles for developing a more inclusive curriculum:

- setting suitable learning challenges
- responding to pupils' diverse learning needs
- overcoming potential barriers to learning and assessment for individuals and groups of pupils (DfEE 1999a, p. 30, 1999b, p. 32).

Curriculum issues and SEN

A standards approach to the curriculum and to assessment can provide useful information, structuring national, regional and local standards of pupil attainment. It also creates a framework against which the inclusion of pupils with SEN into general education and assessment can be judged (and the degree to which alternative curricula and assessment are necessary). Among challenges for teachers is to exercise care and skill in making the agreed curriculum accessible to pupils with SEN or deciding to adapt the curriculum.

Where access is particularly difficult for pupils, the curriculum may have to be modified for two main reasons. The first is so that the lower levels are reachable by pupils with the most severe SEN. The second reason is (if a hierarchical curriculum model is assumed) to enable the steps between the various levels of the curriculum to be made smaller, as appropriate to these pupils.

Different pedagogical approaches may be necessary for pupils with SEN, such as devoting more time than usual to certain aspects of the curriculum, some frequent and discrete teaching of functional skills, more individual teaching and the provision of physical aids and prompts.

It is important to remember the contribution in the National Curriculum of personal, social and health education, which specifically contribute to the development of pupils' personal and social development and can help raise self-esteem. This is considered in a separate chapter.

Assessment issues and SEN

Balancing controlled conditions and flexibility

The assessment of all children is the responsibility of the assessment co-ordinator and in best practice, judging the standards of attainment and progress of pupils with SEN is part of the assessment of all children.

However, when assessing pupils with SEN, the general national structure may not be suitable on its own. Collating information to provide a broad indication of standards of attainment (for example, the test and task levels related to the National Curriculum) may not demonstrate gains in learning which are small or limited to a narrow area of learning.

It is necessary to find a balance between the creation of controlled conditions, and an accurate assessment of the pupil's attainments. On the one hand, controlled conditions are necessary to help ensure that results can be fairly compared with those of others. On the other hand, sufficient flexibility is required to gain an accurate picture of the pupils' attainment level (Rouse and Agbenu, 1998). Accommodation and alternative assessments enable flexibility.

Accommodation

Accommodation for assessment may be summarised in relation to flexibility in: time, setting, presentation, and response. Flexible time may include extending the time allowed for a task, alternating the lengths of the test sessions (e.g. long/short), giving more frequent breaks, and the use of multiple sessions over a number of days. Flexible setting may involve testing a child alone or in a small group, testing him at home with a monitor or in a special education classroom or in a room with special lighting. Alternative presentation formats may embrace Braille or large print, the signing of directions, paraphrasing, audiotaped or video-taped directions or highlighting key words. Alternative response formats include pointing to the response, using a template, responding in sign language, using a computer and allowing answers to be made in a test book (Rouse et al. 2000). An amanuensis may be used.

It is important that accommodation for testing mirrors that for teaching. Accommodation for a particular pupil should be related to his/her particular educational 'needs'. These are reflected in the 'types' of SEN in the guidance for pupil level census returns (Department for Education and Skills 2003a).

A pupil might require accommodation for some parts of a general educational assessment but not need the same accommodation for other parts (or may need different accommodation). Accommodation is intended to level the playing field for pupils with SEN, not to provide them with preferential treatment for assessment (Rouse *et al.* 2000).

Alternative assessments

When alternative assessments are used

Accommodation may be so extensive that the assessment can no longer be regarded as a standard one shared by most children. In these instances, it is necessary to develop alternative forms of assessment that are agreed and as far as possible made similar for the pupils with whom they are used.

PERFORMANCE DESCRIPTIONS (P SCALES)

An example is the Performance Descriptions (P scales) developed for pupils working below level 1 of the National Curriculum and later appended to curriculum guidance for different subjects including English (QCA 2001a), mathematics (QCA 2001b) and personal, social and health education and citizenship (QCA 2001c).

Performance descriptions P1 to P3 are common across all subjects. For example, P1 is 'pupils encounter activities and experiences. They may be passive or resistant. They may show simple reflex responses' (e.g. QCA 2001b, pp. 21–2). From P4 to P8, the scales are subject-specific. For example, P4 for mathematics, shape, space and measure is 'pupils begin to search for objects that have gone out of sight, hearing or touch, demonstrating the beginning of object permanence' (QCA 2001b). In personal, social and health education and citizenship, level P4 is

> pupils express their feelings, needs, likes and dislikes using single elements of communication (words, gestures, signs and symbols). They engage in parallel activity with several others. Pupils follow familiar routines and take part in familiar tasks or activities with support from others. They show an understanding of 'yes' and 'no', and recognise and respond to animated praise or criticism. They begin to respond to the feelings of others
>
> (ibid, p. 23).

PIVATS

Performance Indicators for Value Added Target Setting (PIVATS) were developed under the auspices of Lancashire County Council Education

and Cultural Services Directorate (www.lancashire.gov.uk/education/
pivats/index.asp). PIVATS provides small steps of assessment enabling
judgement of progress to be made between the steps of Performance
Indicators (P scales) and the National Curriculum. Each of the level
descriptions P1(i) to P8 and National Curriculum levels 1C to 4 have
been broken down into five 'stepping stones' bridging each level milestone.

In English, two sections within 'speaking and listening' reflect the
development of expression and comprehension skills within language
and communication. The assessment is linked to the Framework for
teaching the National Literacy Strategy and the National Strategy for
Key Stage 3. PIVATS cover the following:

- speaking and listening – comprehension (P1(i) to P8 and National
  Curriculum level 1C to 8)
- speaking and listening – expression (P1(i) to P8 and National
  Curriculum level 1C to 8)
- reading (P1(i) to P8 and National Curriculum level 1C to 4)
- writing (P1(i) to P8 and National Curriculum level 1C to 4).

The PIVATS for mathematics take account of the framework for teaching the National Numeracy Strategy and the National Strategy for Key
Stage 3. The assessments cover:

- using and applying mathematics (P1(i) to P8 and National
  Curriculum level 1C to 4)
- number (P1(i) to P8 and National Curriculum level 1C to 4)
- shape, space and measures (P1(i) to P8 and National Curriculum
  level 1C to 4).

In science, there are sections for scientific enquiry, life processes and
living things, materials and their properties, and physical processes. The
assessment encompasses:

- scientific enquiry (P1(i) to P8 and National Curriculum level 1 to 4)
- life processes and living things (P1(i) to P8 and National
  Curriculum level 1 to 4)
- materials and their properties (P1(i) to P8 and National Curriculum
  level 1 to 4)
- physical processes (P1(i) to P8 and National Curriculum level 1 to 4).

The PIVATS for personal and social development will be considered in the next chapter.

B-SQUARED

B-squared SEN Publishing is an educational publisher specialising in assessments and workbooks (www.bsquaredsen.co.uk and www.bsquared. co.uk).

B-squared assessment breaks down the programmes of study from the National Curriculum, the P scales, and Foundation Stage documents into finer steps. This helps differentiate pupils' work and target-setting. Assessment files are available in paper form or as a software package. The assessments include the following:

- P Steps Summative Assessment covers English, mathematics and science from P1 to P8 and personal social and health education
- Small Steps Summative Assessment for the English National Curriculum concerns the National Curriculum for English, mathematics and science from level P8 to NC level 5
- Early Steps Summative assessment, based on the foundation document, covers physical development, personal and social development, language and literacy, mathematics, knowledge of the world, and creativity
- Information and Communications Technology assessment extends from P1(i) to level 5 of the National Curriculum
- Personal, Health and Social Education and Citizenship assessment ranges from P1(i) to level 5 of the National Curriculum
- geography assessment extends from P1(i) to level 5 of the National Curriculum
- history assessment goes from P1(i) to level 5 of the National Curriculum
- art assessment covers from P1(i) to level 5 of the National Curriculum.

Performance-based assessments

Another approach, which can be used as an alternative form of assessment, is performance-based assessments allowing pupils to show knowledge and demonstrate skills in a more 'natural' context. This may involve the pupil carrying out a task or preparing a portfolio or exhibition. A portfolio presenting evidence of such work might show entries for students' work in several areas such as 'communication' and 'independence' and provide a summary of his/her job activities and experiences.

A framework for understanding accommodation and alternative assessment

A useful summary of scenarios for assessment and examples of accommodation are envisaged under the Individual with Disabilities in Education Act (IDEA) section 612 enacted in the United States of America (Rouse *et al.* 2000). These can be generalised to other systems including the English system.

The scenarios for assessment are seen as relating to curriculum goals addressed by a pupil which may be:

- educational goals which are general (that is, applying to all pupils)
- educational goals of which some are general and some are pupil-specific (for example, goals to do with independent functioning)
- educational goals which are pupil-specific.

For general educational goals, assessment will involve participation in *all* parts of general educational assessment with either:

a   no accommodation
b   accommodation in some parts
c   accommodation in all parts.

For educational goals, some of which are general and some pupil-specific, assessment will involve participation in *some* parts of general educational assessment with either:

a   some or no accommodation for specific pupil goals;
b   some or no alternative assessments for specific pupil goals.

For specific educational goals, assessment will involve alternative assessments for the goals such as those provided by a portfolio Record of Achievement.

Target-setting

While target-setting, benchmarking and value-added measures have long been used in industry and commerce, it is only relatively recently that attempts have been made to apply aspects of these approaches to the public services including education. Perhaps for this reason, it has sometimes been forgotten that targets represent priorities and that it is unrealistic to have too many of them. Whenever targets are set, there is an 'opportunity cost' as resources are drawn from areas where they might otherwise have been spent. This is why industry managers are very careful not to set too many targets and use target-setting very much as a way of underlining priorities. Targets should be rifle bullets not spread shot. The point of setting targets in education, and the related issues of benchmarking and value-added measures, is to raise standards, including, crucially, standards of attainment.

In England and Wales, strategies for target-setting were developed under the Conservative government and subsequent Labour government (see OfSTED 1996; Barber 1997; Schools Curriculum and Assessment Authority 1997a, 1997b; DfEE 1998, 2001). Schools are statutorily required to set targets in relation to age and expected levels of development. This includes that a pupil at the end of Key Stage 2 of schooling (typically at 11 years old) would be expected to achieve a specified level (currently level 4 of the National Curriculum). Pupils in the final year of compulsory secondary schooling (typically at 16 years old) are expected to achieve certain grades in General Certificate in Secondary Education (GCSE) examinations or their equivalent, for example the General National Vocational Qualification (GNVQ). Schools are statutorily required to set targets for the following:

- the percentage of 11-year-old pupils achieving level 4 of the National Curriculum or better in English and mathematics at the end of Key Stage 2
- the percentage of 16-year-old pupils gaining five or more A* to C grades at GCSE examinations or their equivalent
- the percentage of 16-year-old pupils gaining one or more A* to G grades at GCSE examinations or their equivalent
- the average GCSE/GNVQ score per pupil calculated by assigning each grade a number in an ascending numerical scale according to the higher level of the grade.

National targets are set in relation to these levels. It will be seen that these targets are expressed in terms of levels of attainment of the pupils. To support and encourage the setting of school targets, the government has set national targets for the percentage of pupils nationally to reach the various levels listed above. Schools themselves set targets and inform the LEA. In their turn, LEAs set targets for which they are held to account by the government for schools in their areas. The structure is intended to raise standards of pupil attainment by challenging schools and LEAs to improve.

Potentially negative effects of target-setting on schools working with pupils with SEN

Great interest is generated among parents and others when school results relating to statutory targets are published. Many parents like to see the results in the form of so-called league tables that purport to indicate the success or otherwise of the various schools. It has often been pointed out that a school performing below national expectations may be doing well with its cohort of pupils if it has a lower starting point than other schools. This is of course the 'value added' argument. However, parents looking for the best schools for their children in terms of academic results and an academic environment may be unimpressed by schools doing comparatively well from a lower starting point. Aspiring parents may understandably be more interested in the school offering higher standards of attainment in more 'absolute' terms.

Consequently, the pressure to raise standards is keenly felt by schools. This has led some schools to focus their attentions particularly on pupils who are at the cusp of the threshold that will show up in the respective league tables. Primary schools are eager to ensure that the pupils approaching the end of Key Stage 2 (11 years old) who are nearing level 4 of the National Curriculum in English and mathematics make it past this perceived winning post. Secondary schools are equally concerned that their pupils at 16 years old who are close to getting five A* to C grade GCSEs (the favoured measure of success), do so.

A concern therefore is that, in seeking to reach statutory targets, schools concentrate time and learning resources on the pupils in the middle band of attainment. This can, if the school is not careful, lead to time and other resources being drawn away from pupils who have SEN and who might not be expected to reach the threshold. This applies less to pupils with severe SEN who, in England, have statements of SEN which attract considerable extra funding. It applies more to pupils with less severe SEN at the early years action/school action and early years action plus/school action plus parts of the SEN framework.

Statutory targets as a possible inhibitor of mainstream inclusion

To the extent that an aspect of inclusion is seeking to place more children in mainstream schools and fewer in special schools and other non-mainstream settings, statutory targets may be inhibiting. They may make some mainstream schools reluctant to accept increasing numbers of pupils with SEN at the very time that the government in England appears to be encouraging this.

For example, consider a mainstream school taking on to its roll pupils with moderate learning difficulties. These pupils are by definition behind other pupils in terms of levels of attainment and are unlikely to approach the statutory target threshold. While the pupils with moderate learning difficulties may make progress, this is unlikely to show up on league tables. In the document *Data Collection by Type of Special Educational Needs*, for example, it is noted that 'Pupils with moderate learning difficulties will have attainments significantly below expected levels in most areas of the curriculum, despite appropriate interventions' (DfES 2003a, p. 3).

Schools recognise the need to set targets on an assumption that the parameters do not change once the targets have been set. If inclusion changes the number of children in mainstream schools that have SEN associated with lower levels of attainment, then this will lower the targets that the school sets for all pupils. Yet there is no established machinery for adjusting attainment targets to reflect the inclusion of such pupils with SEN.

Target-setting for pupils with SEN

In the sections above, I considered potentially negative effects on pupils with SEN of the pressure to reach statutory targets for most pupils and maintained that this could draw resources away from pupils with SEN. I also suggested that statutory target-setting for most pupils could inhibit the inclusion of pupils with SEN in mainstream schools. Both issues underline the importance of setting targets for pupils with SEN themselves. In the case of worries about resources being drawn from pupils with SEN, to the extent that schools are held responsible for reaching targets for pupils with SEN, this is likely to counterbalance any shifting of time and resources away from these pupils. In the case of possibly inhibiting inclusion, similarly, having targets for pupils with SEN will demonstrate that progress has been made with the pupils.

Apart from these two concerns, setting targets for pupils with SEN is important in its own right as a way of driving up the standards reached by these pupils. It is difficult to justify why pupils without SEN and pupils with SEN should not both be part of the drive to raise standards of attainment. Yet pupils without SEN are expected to learn and improve so that their standards of attainment rise (target-setting being instrumental in encouraging this). On the other hand, pupils with SEN and their parents sometimes seem to have to settle for the child having his 'needs met' or, even more vacuously, 'celebrating diversity'. If raising standards of attainment is important, it is important for all.

Once the standards of attainment of pupils having SEN are known and recorded, this information can be used to set targets to improve attainment. If a pupil has difficulties relating to literacy or numeracy, targets can be set to encourage higher attainment in these areas. Similarly targets may be set in science and other national curriculum subjects. Targets may also be set in areas of personal, social and behavioural development and these are considered in the next chapter. For a pupil with a disability, attainment targets may be set to help ensure the effectiveness of the school's arrangements to give the pupil access to learning and curriculum (see Chapter 1).

An example of setting targets in literacy

The limitations of targets in Individual Education Plans

This section discusses setting literacy targets for pupils with SEN. But first it is necessary to say something about the limitations of IEP targets. In England and Wales, an IEP is normally maintained for pupils with SEN setting out the special educational needs of the pupil, the provision intended to address them, and individual targets to aim for in a specified time. For example, a target for a pupil with literacy difficulties might be to be able to read a specified list of words in context with 90 per cent accuracy within six weeks, through the strategy of half an hour a day individual tuition focusing on the words.

A difficulty with IEP, however, leaving aside whether they are manageable, is that it is very difficult to know whether the targets set in them are sufficiently ambitious for the pupil and the teachers. Judging the appropriate combination of target and time-scale for achieving it for an individual pupil sets a challenge even for the most experienced teacher. It cannot be known securely whether or not the targets on an IEP are sufficiently stretching or are merely flacid. This issue will be revisited once target-setting has been further considered. Before that, I will outline a five-step approach to setting for pupils with SEN.

Five steps of target-setting

Establishing a baseline of assessment

The first step is, as has already been suggested in the previous section, establishing the attainment levels of the pupils with SEN. The levels of literacy may be assessed in terms of National Curriculum levels. If the pupil is working below level 1 of the National Curriculum, other assessment may be used, such as:

- performance indicators (P scales)
- PIVATS levels
- B-Squared
- standardised tests such as those dev   providers.

Do we need to go into this? ← Detail?

Using comparative data and/or previous

For pupils *without* SEN, the next step would be to look at national and perhaps local or regional data and make a judgement about how well your own school is doing, taking into account factors such as pupils' social background, pupil mobility and other matters. In the case of pupils with SEN the task is more difficult. There is no comprehensive national database of pupils with SEN from which such judgement might be informed. Also, different types of SEN have implications for the standards of attainment of pupils. The standards of literacy attainment for pupils with behavioural, emotional and social difficulties are not comparable with those of pupils with severe learning difficulties. Lancashire has developed a database of over 10,000 pupils with SEN covering schools within Lancashire and other LEAs. The data has been 'sorted' against the PIVATS indicators and groups have been identified against attainment and 'ability', not against areas of SEN. This offers comparative data to help schools setting targets. The compilation of data against ability offers a different approach by setting targets based on what children can do, rather than on what they are unable to do as a result of their type of SEN.

There are local databases that inform judgements on the progress of pupils in relation to several 'types' of SEN such as moderate learning difficulty, an example being the data used by Hampshire LEA (Farrell 2004a, pp. 41–3). There are also extensive databases for some types of SEN such as the data used by the national organisation Equals (www.equals.co.uk) on pupils with severe learning difficulties and other learning difficulties. These can be used to inform judgements about target-setting.

Another approach is for teachers and others to make a judgement predicting likely progress in a specified time, perhaps a year, drawing on the pupil's present and previous attainment and rate of progress. This may be done in consultation with parents. This data can be collected and collated by a senior manager to form the basis for target-setting.

It is very important to remember that the *predictions* of progress made by a good school are not *targets*. Targets lift the aspirations of what pupils could attain higher than what is actually expected. So if a school predicts that of 50 pupils with SEN, say 80 per cent will achieve two P scale steps of progress in reading, a target might be that 90 per cent will achieve this.

Part of the target-setting process involves ensuring that teachers and others who are making initial and subsequent judgements about the levels of a pupils' attainment and achievement, make similar judgements for similar pupils, moderation being part of this process. In a survey conducted by Her Majesty's Inspectors, such moderation was found to be underdeveloped regarding pupils with SEN (OfSTED 2004, p. 3).

Strategies for improving progress

In the process of agreeing targets, it is therefore legitimate to ask how attainment can be raised above the predicted level in a good school doing all it can to improve progress and raise attainment. This relates to the earlier point about targets being priorities. Strategies have to be agreed (and paid for) to enable the targets to be reachable. These strategies might include in our literacy example:

- employing more teaching assistants for literacy
- using information and communications technology better to improve literacy
- ensuring that lesson plans have an explicit literacy element
- buying a more effective scheme to support literacy teaching
- buying more and/or better computer software and ensuring its effective optimum use

- allocating more time to structured and well supported lit teaching
- training staff better in tried and tested literacy interventions
- involving parents to help reach the targets.

Part of the process of developing suitable strategies to ensure that agreed targets are reached is to explicitly allocate the time and money involved. It should be clear who is responsible for making sure the target is reached.

Revisiting IEP targets

Once the targets are agreed, any targets set in an IEP are revisited and improved so that IEPs reflect the higher aspirations (and practical steps to realise the aspirations) the school has agreed. The progress towards them is monitored so that fine-tuning can take place to ensure that targets are reached, to check where the time comes from to manage this, and where the money for equipment or whatever else is proposed comes from and so on.

This strengthens the use of IEPs so that their targets are supported by data from the school as a whole and by data from a similar cohort of pupils in another school where benchmarking is used (see the section on benchmarking below).

Evaluating the impact of strategies

During the time in which the targets are being pursued, and certainly at the end of the target-setting period, the effectiveness of the strategies used to help reach the targets should be evaluated. This will of course be informed by whether or not the targets were reached. The school will consider which strategies or aspects of strategies have been helpful and which have not. Care has to be taken where cohorts are very small as inferences could be made without a secure foundation.

Schools routinely use target-setting to inform performance management, although a survey reported in 2004 and focusing on target-setting for pupils with SEN, found that schools do not always link the performance of teachers to evidence of improved pupil performance. Also, where performance management was directly related to professional development, it contributed significantly to school improvement (OfSTED 2004, p. 25).

Benchmarking

In the earlier section on target-setting, the question of comparing the attainment of the pupils with SEN in a school with information from elsewhere was mentioned. This relates to benchmarking. I mentioned that there are some large databases such as that used by the Equals organisation (www. equals.co.uk). There is also LEA data.

If benchmarking is used to inform a school of how it can do better, a useful approach is to work with another school with a similar cohort of pupils with SEN. For example, if two primary schools are comparing the attainment of the pupils considered to have SEN in their respective schools, it would make sense if the cohorts were of similar size, starting from similar levels of attainment, having similar types of SEN and within the same age group. If most pupils in the two schools were considered to have literacy difficulties, the two schools might usefully work together in their target-setting process.

The progress of pupils in each school may be compared over an agreed period, say, a year. If one school makes better progress than the other, then the two schools can evaluate their results and learn from what has worked well and what has not. This involves a professional dialogue and assumes that some staff from each school can meet, perhaps once a term, to review progress. For this reason it is probably better to think in terms of schools within easy travelling distance of each other. E-mail contact is no substitute for professional contact, in-depth discussion and seeing another school's strategies in context.

Value-added measures

Drawing on benchmarking information, a judgement about the value that a school has added to a child's educational progress is a difficult and subtle one particularly when it concerns pupils with SEN. It can be related to what was said earlier about the difference between the predicted progress expected for a pupil and the extra that is developed with the help of targets set at higher levels than would normally be predicted. This difference, supported by effective strategies, relates to the value that the school adds.

When the progress indicated by pupils reaching targets is compared with the progress of pupils with SEN coming from similar starting points in similar schools, and compares favourably, this is strong indication of value added. Such evidence of good progress may then be related to the cost involved when estimating the cost-effectiveness of interventions.

Case study 3 Pear Tree School – pupils' progress

This case study illustrates the use of P scales in assessing the progress in writing of pupils in a special school, Pear Tree School in Lancashire. The school provides for pupils aged three to 19 years that have severe learning difficulties or profound and multiple learning difficulties.

One strategy that the school used to judge how well it was doing in raising standards was to collate the assessments in writing for all pupils over a three-year period. This data indicated that the pupils were underachieving across different age groups and irrespective of whether they were assessed as having severe or profound and multiple learning difficulties. At the time the school started the initiative, it had baseline data and two years of subsequent data using the PIVATS (version 1) assessments. This indicated that for the majority of pupils, the score they achieved in writing was consistently lower than that in other areas and in some instances considerably lower. For example, three pupils scored level P5 in writing but scored between level P7 and National Curriculum level 1B in all other areas. (When the original P scales were revised, and the PIVATS had to be similarly revised to produce PIVATS version 2, the school effectively had to start again with its assessments to ensure reliability in comparing scores over time.) A further indication that pupils were underachieving in writing was the judgements of an OfSTED inspection in 2001 which judged progress in writing by ages 7, 11, 16 and 19 to be all 'C'. By comparison, speaking and listening progress; personal, social and health education progress; and progress against other personal targets set at annual reviews or in IEP for these ages was judged to be 'A'. Reading progress was judged to be 'B'.

Most pupils worked between levels P4 to P6 in writing. But about 20 of the secondary-aged pupils were working between levels P7 and level 1 of the National Curriculum. The main question the school was asking in considering this information was why pupils were underachieving across the age ranges. The fact that older pupils were reaching higher levels was put down to age and maturation.

The school considered the possible reasons for the underperformance in writing. These included:

- whether the pupils not considered to be progressing had sufficient time for writing and pre-writing activities
- whether the teaching methods were appropriate
- whether the resources used were suitable
- whether the expectations of teachers and others were high
  enough in relation to pupils with poor fine motor skills.

An audit of the school's provision was carried out leading to several changes in the school's approach to the above issues. These
changes were:

- a new policy for writing and a new scheme of work.
  Developing these focused the school's attention on its
  approach to the teaching of writing across the school and the
  priority it placed on this for individual children. Discussion
  with staff when the policy was being formulated resulted in
  everyone affirming a commitment to providing more opportunities for the development and practice of writing skills,
  especially for those children who could make progress in this
  area. It ensured consistency regarding the school's approach
  to the teaching of writing throughout the school and across
  the curriculum. The new scheme of work replaced the more
  ad hoc approach to the teaching of writing, with a structure
  and a framework including detailed guidelines and teaching
  strategies for each key stage. Again, staff discussions in for-
  mulating the scheme focused attention on what would be
  taught, the teaching strategies to be used and the additional
  resources that would be needed if the school were to provide
  enhanced opportunities for writing across the curriculum.
- the school ensured that its resources, including information and
  communication technology software, were age-appropriate.
- grouping arrangements were reconsidered. As a result, pupils
  were grouped within and across classes within the same or the
  next key stage with other pupils of similar prior attainment to
  give enhanced opportunities to develop their skills in this
  area.
- lesson plans gave attention to writing in every lesson.
- lesson plans were regularly evaluated. These now include

identified learning outcomes with a writing focus for each pupil and all teachers are encouraged to provide writing opportunities in each area of the curriculum whenever possible. The progress the pupil makes against the learning outcomes is evaluated by the staff working with them to inform future expectations. Outcomes set for the pupil are monitored by the deputy head teacher to ensure that they are sufficiently challenging.

- a teaching approach was established that was related to a developmental view of language acquisition and which used topics and themes seeking to help the pupils generalise the skills of writing, reading, speaking and listening.
- profiles of the attainment and progress of individual pupils and of groups of pupils were used to measure progress and set targets for the future.

An evaluation of the changes indicated that the progress of pupils had improved. The school recognises that the cohorts concerned are small and that there are difficulties posed in tracking pupils because of the changes in PIVATS. This meant that a significant amount of teacher moderation had to be done when converting scores from PIVATS 1 to PIVATS 2. Nevertheless consideration of the PIVATS 2 scores for July 2003 of the three pupils mentioned earlier whose writing scores were significantly different to other achievements, showed that they had improved to level P7. This represents a rate of progress significantly greater than that in other areas. In 2004, Pear Tree worked with two or three special schools to examine data across the three schools and the progress that similar pupils made in each school.

It will be seen that the approach used by Pear Tree has the strength of identifying areas of concern based on a focus on standards of attainment, achievement and progress. The school then carried out an audit to refine its concerns and seek areas for improvement. It developed and implemented changes that would be expected to lead to improvements. It then evaluated the changes in a continuing cycle of improvement.

(From information kindly supplied by Pear Tree School, Lancashire)

Summary/conclusion

This chapter outlined the development of the National Curriculum and national assessment in England. I considered curriculum issues and SEN, and assessment and SEN, in particular 'accommodation' and alternative assessments. The chapter looked at matters arising for target-setting, in particular the potentially negative effects of target-setting on schools working with pupils with SEN, and statutory targets as a possible inhibitor of mainstream inclusion. I explained procedures for target-setting with pupils having SEN giving an example of setting literacy targets. The chapter touched on the approaches of benchmarking and value-added measures for pupils with SEN. The case study illustrated the use of P scales for improving writing skills in a special school.

Thinking points

Readers may wish to consider:

• whether the approach outlined in this chapter might reinvigorate target-setting and benchmarking in some schools
• the practicalities of working with other schools to develop a professional dialogue examining effective provision for pupils with SEN.

Key texts

Farrell, M. (2003a) *Understanding Special Educational Needs: A Guide for Student Teachers,* London: RoutledgeFalmer.

Although this book is aimed mainly at student teachers and newly qualified teachers, many experienced teachers report finding it a useful review of some of the current issues in SEN. Chapter 5, 'Raising educational achievement and the use of individual education plans', complements some of what is said in the present chapter but with more emphasis on the role of the IEP.

Personal and social development and behaviour and target-setting

Introduction

This chapter looks at the importance of personal and social development and behaviour. It considers the National Curriculum and the non-statutory framework in terms of the foundation stage and Key Stages 1 to 4. I examine ways of adapting and encouraging access to PSHE and citizenship by using and refining the National Curriculum framework, focusing particularly on pupils with learning difficulties and by considering pupils with behavioural, emotional and social difficulties. The chapter then turns to assessing personal and social development using PSHE and citizenship structures. Finally, the chapter examines target-setting and personal and social development.

The importance of personal and social development and behaviour

I made it clear when defining standards of attainment and achievement earlier in the book that standards of achievement are taken to include personal and social development. This also encompasses behaviour and emotional development. The importance of this for all pupils including pupils with SEN will be apparent. Such development is valuable in itself. Also, to the extent that personal and social development contribute to self-esteem and motivation, it is likely to have a positive effect on attainment in academic subjects of the curriculum.

A positive underpinning structure for personal and social development and high expectations of behaviour in a school are important when educating pupils with social, emotional and behavioural difficulties. Such structures are assumed to have been secure and to have had all the impact that can be expected before more specific interventions are considered such as psychotherapy, behaviour modification or systems approaches.

The National Curriculum and non-statutory framework

The foundation stage and Key Stages 1 to 4

This section examines personal, social and emotional development and early learning goals in the foundation stage of education; PSHE and citizenship at Key Stages 1 and 2; PSHE and citizenship at Key Stages 3 and 4.

Personal, social and emotional development and early learning goals in the foundation stage

Work planned in the foundation stage of education (which applies to children from age three years to the end of the reception year in primary school) should be based on specified areas of learning and on the early learning goals. Personal, social and emotional development (PSED) is one of the six areas of learning and includes 'dispositions and attitudes, self-confidence and self-esteem, making relationships, behaviour and self-control, self-care, sense of community' (Office for Standards of Education 1999, p. 2).

The expectations for most children by the end of the foundation stage are as follows:

- *Dispositions and attitudes:* children keen to learn; developing confidence and independence; able to concentrate well when their interest is engaged.
- *Self confidence and self-esteem:* an interested response to events which are significant to the children and an ability to show their feelings.
- *Making relationships:* generally good relationships with peers and positive relationships with adults when working in small and larger groups; an understanding of the basic rules that make for harmonious groups, such as taking turns and working together when appropriate.
- *Behaviour and self-control:* a developing knowledge of what is right and wrong; some understanding of the consequences of their actions for themselves and others.

- *Self care*: independence in dressing and undressing and in taking care of their personal hygiene; an ability to select and use activities and resources with independence.
- *Sense of community*: ability to show empathy with an understanding of others, and have a developing respect for their own culture and beliefs as well as those of other people (ibid., p. 9).

Personal, social and health education and the National Curriculum at Key Stages 1 and 2

The National Curriculum Handbook for Primary Teachers in England (Department for Education and Employment/Qualifications and Curriculum Authority 1999a) sets PSHE and citizenship within the context of promoting spiritual, moral, social and cultural development across the National Curriculum. It states that:

> All National Curriculum subjects provide opportunities to promote pupils' spiritual, moral, social and cultural development. Explicit opportunities to promote pupils' development in these areas are provided in religious education and the non-statutory framework for personal, social and health education (PSHE) and citizenship at key stages 1 and 2. A significant contribution is made by school ethos, effective relationships throughout the school, collective worship and other curriculum areas.
>
> (ibid., p. 19)

The *Handbook* provides non-statutory guidelines 'to help schools establish coherence and consistency, and to promote curriculum continuity and progression in pupils' learning in PSHE and citizenship' (ibid., p. 20).

Readers wishing to refresh their memory of these guidelines for Key Stages 1 and 2 will find these in the *Handbook* on pages 136–41. Essentially, PSHE and citizenship aim to 'help to give pupils the knowledge, skills and understanding they need to lead confident, healthy, independent lives and to become informed, active responsible citizens' (ibid., p. 136).

The guidance continues:

> Pupils are encouraged to take part in a wide range of activities and experiences across and beyond the curriculum, contributing fully to the life of their school and communities. In doing so they learn to

recognise their own worth, work well with others and become increasingly responsible for their own learning. They reflect on their experiences and understand how they are developing personally and socially, tackling many of the spiritual, moral, social and cultural issues that are part of growing up. They also find out about the main political and social institutions that affect their lives and about their responsibilities, rights and duties as individuals and members of communities. They learn to understand and respect our common humanity, diversity and differences so that they can go on to form the effective, fulfilling relationships that are an essential part of life and learning.

(ibid., p. 136)

The guidelines for both Key Stages 1 and 2 cover knowledge, skills and understanding under four headings. In the guidance, under each heading is a list of what pupils should be taught. Examples are given below from Keys Stages 1 and 2.

- Developing confidence and responsibility and making the most of their abilities

  - KS1, pupils should be taught 'to recognise what they like and dislike, what is fair and unfair, and what is right and wrong' and 'to recognise, name and deal with their feelings in a positive way' (ibid., p. 137).
  - KS2, pupils should be taught 'to recognise their worth as individuals by identifying positive things about themselves and their achievements, seeing their mistakes, making amends and setting personal goals' (ibid., p. 139).

- Preparing to play an active role as citizens

  - For example, pupils should be taught 'to agree to follow rules for their group and classroom, and understand how rules help them' (ibid., p. 137).
  - KS2, pupils should be taught 'to realise the consequences of anti-social and aggressive behaviours, such as bullying and racism, on individuals and communities' (ibid., p. 139).

- Developing a healthy, safer lifestyle

  - KS1, pupils should be taught 'how to make simple choices that improve their health and well-being' (ibid., p. 137).

- KS2, pupils should be taught 'what makes a healthy lifestyle, including the benefits of exercise and healthy eating, what effects [sic] mental health, and how to make informed choices' (ibid., p. 140).

• Developing good relationships and respecting the difference between people

- KS1, pupils should be taught 'that there are different types of teasing and bullying, that bullying is wrong, and how to get help to deal with bullying' (ibid., p. 138).
- KS2, pupils should be taught 'to recognise and challenge stereotypes' and 'that differences and similarities between people arise from a number of factors, including cultural, ethnic, racial and religious diversity, gender and disability' (ibid., p. 140).

Such knowledge, skills and understanding should be taught through a breadth of curricular opportunities. At KS1 these include to 'take and share responsibility [for example for their own behaviour; by helping to make classroom rules and following them; by looking after pets well]' (ibid., p. 138). At KS2 they include 'participate [for example, in the school's decision- making process …]' (ibid., p. 141).

There are no National Curriculum attainment targets for PSHE or citizenship at Key Stages 1 and 2 because the subject guidance is non-statutory.

Personal, social and health education at KS3 and 4

The National Curriculum Handbook for Secondary Teachers in England (Department for Education and Employment/Qualifications and Curriculum Authority 1999b) sets PSHE and citizenship within the context of promoting SMSC development across the National Curriculum in the same way that the primary phase guidance does. The only difference is that it refers to PSHE only and not citizenship, which is treated separately because at KS3 and 4 citizenship is a statutory subject (see Department for Education and Employment/Qualifications and Curriculum Authority 1999b, p. 21).

The *Handbook* provides non-statutory guidelines 'to help schools establish coherence and consistency, and to promote curriculum continuity and progression in pupils' learning in PSHE. These complement the statutory requirements for citizenship …' (ibid., p. 21).

The guidelines for Key Stages 3 and 4 are in the *Handbook* on pages 188–194. Essentially, PSHE aims to 'help pupils to lead confident, healthy, and responsible lives as individuals and members of society' (ibid., p. 188).

The guidance continues:

> Through work in lesson time and in a wide range of activities across and beyond the curriculum, pupils gain practical knowledge and skills to help them live healthily and deal with the spiritual, moral, social and cultural issues they face as they approach adulthood. PSHE gives pupils opportunities to reflect on their experiences and how they are developing. It helps them to understand and manage responsibly a wider range of relationships as they mature, and to show respect for the diversity of, and differences between, people. It also develops pupils' well being and self esteem, encouraging belief in their ability to succeed and enabling them to take responsibility for their learning and future choice of course and career. PSHE at key stages 3 and 4 builds on pupils' own experiences and on work at key stages 1 and 2 and complements citizenship in the curriculum, which covers public policy dilemmas related to health, law and family.
>
> (ibid., p. 188)

The guidelines for both Key Stages 3 and 4 cover knowledge, skills and understanding under three headings. In the guidance, under each heading, is listed what pupils should be taught. Examples are given below.

- Developing confidence and responsibility and making the most of their abilities

  - KS3, pupils should be taught 'to recognise the stages of emotions associated with loss and change caused by death, divorce, separation and new family members, and how to deal positively with the strength of their feelings in different situations' (ibid., p. 189).
  - KS4, pupils should be taught 'to be aware of how others see them, manage praise and criticism, and success and failure in a positive way and learn from the experience' (ibid., p. 193).

- Developing a healthy, safer lifestyle

  - KS3, pupils should be taught 'basic facts and laws, including school rules, about alcohol and tobacco, illegal substances and the risks of misusing prescribed drugs' (ibid., p. 189).

- KS4, pupils should be taught 'the causes, symptoms and treatment for stress and depression, and to identify strategies for prevention and management' (ibid., p. 192).

• Developing good relationships and respecting the difference between people

- KS3, pupils should be taught 'to resist pressure to do wrong, to recognise when others need help and how to support them' (ibid., p. 190).
- KS4, pupils should be taught 'to be aware of exploitation in relationships' (ibid., p. 193).

Such knowledge, skills and understanding should be taught through a breadth of curricular opportunities. At KS3 these include opportunities to 'develop relationships [for example, by working together in a range of groups and social settings with their peers and others; ...] (ibid., p. 190). At KS4 they include 'consider social and moral dilemmas [for example, young parenthood, genetic engineering, attitudes to the law]' (ibid., p. 194).

There are no National Curriculum attainment targets for PSHE at Key Stages 3 and 4 because the subject guidance is non-statutory.

Citizenship at KS3 and 4

The National Curriculum Handbook for Secondary Teachers in England (Department for Education and Employment/Qualifications and Curriculum Authority 1999b) describes the importance of citizenship.

Citizenship gives pupils the knowledge, skills and understanding to play an effective role in society at local, national and international levels. It helps them to become informed, thoughtful and responsible citizens who are aware of their duties and rights. It promotes their spiritual, moral, social and cultural development, making them more self-confident and responsible both in and beyond the classroom. It encourages pupils to play a helpful part in the life of their schools, neighbourhoods, communities and the wider world. It also teaches them about our economy and democratic institutions and values; encourages respect for different national, religious and ethnic identities; and develops pupils' ability to reflect on issues and take part in discussions. Citizenship is complemented by the framework for personal, social and health education at key stages 3 and 4.

(ibid., p. 183)

At Key Stages 3 and 4, the programmes of study for citizenship fall under three headings, and examples of what pupils should be taught under each is given below.

- Knowledge and understanding about becoming informed citizens

    - KS3, pupils should be taught 'the importance of resolving conflict fairly' (ibid., p. 184).
    - KS4, pupils should be taught about 'the legal and human rights and responsibilities underpinning society and how they relate to citizens, including the role and operation of the criminal and civil justice systems' (ibid., p. 185).

- Developing skills of enquiry and communication

    - KS3, pupils should be taught to 'think about topical political, spiritual, moral, social and cultural issues, problems and events by analysing information and its sources, including ICT-based sources' (ibid., p. 184).
    - KS4, pupils should be taught to 'contribute to group and exploratory class discussions, and take part in formal debates' (ibid., p. 185).

- Developing skills of participation and responsible action

    - KS3, pupils should be taught to 'negotiate, decide and take part in both school and community-based activities' (ibid., p. 184).
    - KS4, pupils should be taught to 'express, justify and defend orally and in writing a personal opinion about ... issues, problems and events' (ibid., p. 185).

The attainment targets for citizenship are expressed as end of key stage descriptions. The expectations are intended to match the level of demand in other subjects and are 'broadly equivalent to levels 5 and 6 at key stage 3' (ibid., attainment target appendix, p. 49). Both the end of Key Stage 3 description and the end of Key Stage 4 description reflect the work expected in the programme of study.

Adapting and encouraging access to PSHE and citizenship

Using and refining the framework

The foundation stage, the framework for PSHE and citizenship at Key Stages 1 and 2 and the framework for PSHE and the curriculum for citizenship at Key Stages 3 and 4 provide a structure for these aspects of learning and development. This is as important for pupils with SEN as it is for pupils who are not identified as having SEN.

For many pupils, their personal and social development and behaviour are well supported by such a structure. For some pupils with SEN, such a structure may not be sufficient to encourage and support personal and social development. For example, pupils with moderate learning difficulties, severe learning difficulties, or profound and multiple learning difficulties may need particular support. Pupils with behavioural, emotional and social difficulties, by definition are likely to need emotional and other support and specific interventions if they are to experience the sort of personal and social development indicated in the structure considered earlier. This section therefore looks at these issues.

Personal, social and health education and citizenship for pupils with learning difficulties

A series of guidelines developed for pupils with learning difficulties (moderate learning difficulties, severe learning difficulties, profound and multiple learning difficulties) includes guidance relating to personal, social and health education and citizenship for pupils with learning difficulties (Qualification and Curriculum Authority 2001c).

The guidelines indicate ways in which the PSHE framework and citizenship programmes of study can be modified, for example by choosing material from an earlier key stage or from more than one key stage (ibid., p. 4). They interpret the requirements of the framework and programme of study to make them relevant to the pupils with SEN they are considering. For example, in relation to the aspect of PSHE concerning 'developing confidence and responsibility and making the most of their abilities', the guidance focuses on self-concept, self-awareness, self-esteem and self-knowledge. With regard to self-knowledge, it is suggested that 'Some pupils with learning difficulties may be dependent on staff to help them interpret their preferences' (ibid., p. 5).

Regarding sex and relationship education, it is suggested that 'pupils with learning difficulties may need to specifically learn things which other pupils learn incidentally, for example, what being 'private' actually means' (ibid., p. 6).

Examples of opportunities and activities across all key stages are given, for example in helping ensure that 'pupils have opportunities to take and share responsibility', the pupil may 'lead the way to different areas in the school and show visitors around the school' (ibid., p. 8).

Further examples of opportunities and activities are provided in relation to Key Stages 1 through 4. For example, a possible Key Stage 2 activity intended to help prepare the pupil for change and help him cope with it, the pupil may 'experience deliberate changes in regular routines, for example, lunch in the food technology kitchen rather than in the school dining room' (ibid., p. 14).

Pupils with behavioural, emotional and social difficulties

Pupils with behavioural, emotional and social difficulties (BESD) are by definition likely to be less well developed in their emotional and social development and their behaviour may be disruptive or otherwise inappropriate.

I suggested in Chapter 3 that BESD may also be understood in terms of standards of achievement in the broad sense of emotional, behavioural and social development and attitudes to learning. While it is not practical to relate behaviour, emotional development and social development to national tests and tasks, I suggested that, underpinning judgements that a child has BESD is some form of comparison with what can be reasonably expected of children of the same age. This may be related to standardised assessments of development, the judgements of teachers, parents, psychologists and others informed by their experience of other children. I emphasised that such judgements are somewhat subjective and that they are informed by the quality of the teaching and the behaviour management and pastoral approaches of the school and by other factors.

In the particular case of pupils with attention deficit hyperactivity disorder (ADHD), the guidance on 'types' of SEN provided by the Department for Education and Skills to help with pupil census forms states that they 'may have reduced attention and impulsivity'(DfES, 2003, p. 4). Such behaviour indicating reduced attention and impulsivity may be taken as indicating, in developmental or achievement terms, lower levels of attention than is expected in a child of the same age.

Therefore when interventions are proposed for pupils with BESD, it is expected that in the longer term, there will be improvements in personal, emotional and social development and behaviour. Of course, this is not to suggest that the only way of seeing and addressing BESD is through concentrating on the development directly. It may be that a particular child will benefit from psychotherapy or some other intervention in which the initial focus is not on behaviour but on some interpretation of internal states and perceptions. Neither is this to ignore the anguish and abuse that is sometime associated with BESD. Intervention with the child, his family and others may take these into account.

However, there is a contribution that can be made educationally and this lies in the area of teaching, learning and creating good role models of personal and social development and behaviour.

Assessing personal and social development

Assessing personal and social development using PSHE and citizenship structures

The structures for PSHE and citizenship are limited in what they offer in assessing development in these areas. In citizenship end of key stage descriptions are provided related to the programme of study but these apply only to the end of Key Stages 3 and 4 and are very broad.

With PSHE, it is understandable perhaps that there are no attainment targets. It is particularly difficult to envisage personal development, for example, as a hierarchical arrangement of skills. Much depends on sensitivities to other people and situations. It is not surprising that there is a General Certificate in Secondary Education in citizenship, but it would be difficult to imagine a GCSE in personal development. If someone failed such an examination, would it mean that they were no longer a person?

Assessing PSHE for pupils with moderate, severe or profound and multiple learning difficulties

An attempt has been made to provide performance descriptions for PSHE and citizenship for pupils with 'learning difficulties' (in this context meaning pupils with moderate learning difficulties, severe learning difficulties or profound and multiple learning difficulties). These can be used, among other things, to 'record pupils' overall development and achievement ...' (Qualification and Curriculum Authority 2001c, p. 26).

An example is performance description 4:

> Pupils express their feelings, needs, likes and dislikes using single
> elements of communication (words, gestures, signs or symbols).
> They engage in parallel activity with several others. Pupils follow
> familiar routines and take part in familiar tasks and activities with
> support from others. They show an understanding of 'yes' and 'no',
> and recognise and respond to animated praise or criticism. They
> begin to respond to the feelings of others, for example, matching
> their emotions or becoming upset (ibid., p. 27).

More specific assessments

In trying to assess personal and social development and behaviour,
including BESD, the approach is sometimes more specific. It includes
seeking to assess social skills, 'emotional literacy', coping strategies and
other features of development.

For example, among tests produced by NFER-Nelson (www.nfer-
nelson.co.uk) are the following.

Connors' Rating Scale: Revised

C. KEITH CONNORS

This assessment is intended for use by educational psychologists to evaluate problem behaviours including attention deficit hyperactivity
disorder using reports from parents, teachers and the child or young person himself. For use with children from three to 17 years old, the test is
administered to individuals and may be used to measure changes
brought about by interventions and to evaluate intervention strategies.

Social Skills Training: Enhancing Social Competence with Children and Adolescents

SUSAN H. SPENCE

This assessment may be used by teachers, educational psychologists,
counsellors and social workers. It is for children and young people aged
five to 18 years and may be used as an individual or a group test. It is
intended to help assess social competence and to enable the design of
suitable intervention programmes. The programme particularly aims to
change negative thinking patterns and to raise self-esteem.

Emotional Literacy – Assessment and Intervention

SOUTHAMPTON PSYCHOLOGY SERVICE: EDITOR ANDREW FAUPEL

This may be administered by special educational needs co-ordinators, teachers, educational psychologists, counsellors, learning mentors and professionals in Pupil Referral Units. For children and young people aged seven to 16, it may by administered individually or to a group. It aims to identify the status of pupils' emotional literacy and suggests, as necessary, follow-up activities for intervention that can be used at home or school. Reassessment can be used to monitor progress and help the teacher to judge the effect of an intervention.

Adolescent Coping Scale

ERICA FRYDENBERG AND RAMON LEWIS

For use by teachers, special educational needs co-ordinators, researchers and educational psychologists, the assessment is intended for adolescents aged 12 to 18 years. It is an individually administered self-report questionnaire taking between two and 15 minutes to complete. It seeks to help adolescents improve their range of coping strategies by encouraging them to think about how they have dealt with past difficulties and develop alternative strategies to improve their competence in dealing with stressful situations.

Insight

ELIZABETH MORRIS

This resource may be used by teachers, special educational needs co-ordinators, child-care workers, counsellors and learning mentors, and applies to children and young people aged three to 18 years. The 'Self-Esteem Indicator' is completed by the administrator, is untimed and suitable for individual or group use. It is available in three levels, pre-school, primary and secondary. The indicator sees self-esteem in terms of the pupil's sense of self, belonging and personal power. The materials can be used for reassessment and the secondary material is suitable for use with pupils with BESD in mainstream and special schools and in pupil referral units.

   Among tests produced by The Psychological Corporation (www.tpc-international.com) are the following:

Beck Youth Inventories™ of Emotional and Social Impairment

JUDITH S. BECK, AARON T. BECK AND JOHN JOLLY (2001)

These provide an evaluation of children's emotional and social impairment through the use of five self-report inventories that can be used individually or together. The inventories assess symptoms of depression, anger, anxiety, disruptive behaviour and self-concept for children aged seven to 14 years. Each inventory comprises 20 statements about the thoughts, feelings and behaviours associated with emotional and social impairment in the age range of the assessment. The children describe how frequently the statement has been true for them.

The Self Image Profiles (SIP)

RICHARD J. BUTLER (2001)

The SIPs are short self-report measures assessing the child's theory of self. SIP-C applies to children aged seven to 11 years while SIP-A is for adolescents aged 12 to 16 years. The SIP provides a visual display relating to self image indicating the way the person completing it construes himself/herself as (s)he completes it. A SIP measure of self-esteem is estimated by the discrepancy between ratings of 'How I am' and 'How I would like to be'. The assessment is used in educational contexts by teachers, specialist support service staff and educational psychologists. It has United Kingdom norms.

Target-setting and personal and social development

Setting targets using the PSHE performance descriptions

Targets can be set for improving personal and social development to the extent that these are reflected in the PSHE performance descriptors. With a group of, say, 30 pupils having severe learning difficulties, each pupil is first assessed according to a P level. Teachers and others working with each pupil then predict the standards of achievements the pupil will reach in a specified time, perhaps a year. Department for Education and Skills guidelines suggest that pupils should attain at least two 'levels' within each key stage. This is of concern because for young children with severe learning difficulties who are operating within P scale levels, achieving one P level of progress may represent considerable success. PIVATS allows smaller steps of progress to be recorded.

These predictions are collated and it is seen that, say 80 per cent of the total pupils are expected to progress at least one P level while perhaps 40 per cent of the total are predicted to progress by two P levels. Members of the senior management team (including the special educational needs co-ordinator) review the predictions with the head teacher and make a judgement on what a realistic and challenging target will be over and above the predicted progress.

It may be that 100 per cent of the pupils progress at least one P level and 45 per cent progress at least two P levels. These proposed targets are put to the staff whose main responsibility it will be to see that the targets are reached. A debate is likely to take place about how the progress is to be achieved and this may involve allocating more time to work and support related to the achievement of the target. It may also involve spending money that otherwise would have been spent on something else, what economists call 'opportunity costs'. This is the sense in which targets are priorities.

The next P level that is being aimed for will indicate the type of work and support needed in particular instances. For example, one might be aiming for children to reach P level 5:

> Pupils take part in work or play involving two or three others. They maintain interactions and take turns in a small group with some support. Pupils combine two elements of communication to express their feelings, needs and choices. They join in discussions by responding appropriately (vocalising, using gestures, symbols and signing) to simple questions about familiar events or experiences, for example, 'What does the baby need?'
> (Qualification and Curriculum Authority 2001c, p. 27)

Reaching this target will require staff to set up situations regularly in which the pupils engage in play with two or three others. It will involve encouraging, praising and supporting interactions. It will require the teaching and modelling of turn taking, and so on. It is not assumed that this sort of teaching would never have happened without the target, but the target helps ensure that it takes place systematically and accountably. Where many pupils are aiming for the same target, much of the work can take place in groups.

Progress towards the targets can be monitored to allow steps to be taken if progress is not rapid enough.

PIVATS

Targets may also be set in a similar way using Performance Indicators for Value-Added Target Setting (www.lancashire.gov.uk/education/pivats/index.asp) or PIVATS developed under the auspices of Lancashire County Council Education and Cultural Services Directorate. These provide small steps of assessment enabling judgement of progress to be made between the steps of Performance Indicators (P scales) and the National Curriculum. Each of the level descriptions P1(i) to P8 and National Curriculum levels 1C to 4 have been broken down into five 'stepping stones' bridging each level milestone. PIVATS have been developed for English, mathematics, science and personal and social and health education.

In personal and social development, PIVATS draw on P scales for personal and social development (DfEE 1998) and criteria for measuring emotional and behavioural development (QCA 2001d). The assessments cover:

- interacting and working with others (conduct behaviour) (PSD1 to PSD16)
- independence and organisational skills (PSD1 to PSD16)
- attention (learning behaviour) (PSD1 to PSD16).

B-squared

Targets may be set using B-squared assessments (www.bsquaredsen.co.uk and www.bsquared.co.uk). These break down into finer steps the programmes of study from the National Curriculum, the P scales, and Foundation Stage documents. The assessments include:

- P Steps Summative assessment includes Personal, Social and Health Education from P1 to P8
- Early Steps Summative assessment, based on the foundation document, includes personal and social development
- Personal, Health and Social Education and Citizenship assessment ranges from P1(i) to level 5 of the National Curriculum.

Using an assessment to determine and improve achievement: self-esteem

A similar approach can be taken with other more specific dimensions, for example, self-esteem. This can be aided by the Secondary Insight materials to which I referred in the previous section (Morris 2002a, 2002b, 2002c).

Summary/conclusion

This chapter looked at the importance of personal and social development and behaviour. It considered the National Curriculum and the non-statutory framework in terms of the foundation stage and Key Stages 1 to 4. I examined ways of adapting and encouraging access to PSHE and citizenship by using and refining the National Curriculum framework, focusing particularly on pupils with learning difficulties and by considering pupils with behavioural, emotional and social difficulties. The chapter then turned to assessing personal and social development using PSHE and citizenship structures. Finally, the chapter examined target-setting and personal and social development.

Thinking points

Readers may wish to consider with reference to their particular school:

- the extent to which there is a coherent approach to the development of Personal, Social and Health Education and Citizenship (PSHCE), drawing on National Curriculum structures and guidance
- the appropriateness and effectiveness of the assessment of personal, social and emotional development and how it is used to enhance such development for example through target-setting.

Key texts

It is difficult to recommend one or two key texts for this chapter and a helpful strategy might be to consult the range of sources mentioned, including some of the individual assessments. This should help ensure that a particular school has a comprehensive approach to education for PSHCE and a range of assessments to inform provision and help further develop social, personal and emotional development.

Chapter 6

Inclusion

Introduction

I distinguish between integration and inclusion. The chapter then outlines three types of inclusion: social inclusion, the inclusion of pupils already in mainstream schools, and the balance of pupils with SEN in mainstream and special schools. Regarding the latter, the chapter argues for an approach that takes into account the standards of pupils' attainment reached in the venue that provides education. This may be solely or predominantly a mainstream school, a special school, a pupil referral unit or another venue. I have previously referred to this approach as 'educational inclusion' to indicate that the quality of education as reflected in standards in the widest sense is central (Farrell 2000). Because this expression does not sufficiently distinguish its essential focus on standards from other approaches relating to inclusion in an educational setting, I wish instead to adopt the term 'optimal education' in this chapter.

A case study illustrates the use of information on the attainment and progress of pupils with SEN to inform judgements concerning inclusion of pupils in mainstream schools.

Defining inclusion

Distinguishing between inclusion and integration

The term inclusion has been used in many different ways. One starting point in trying to establish an understanding of the concept is to compare and contrast it with the term 'integration'. Both terms are to do with provision for pupils with SEN in mainstream schools. Integration has been characterised as assuming that the mainstream school system remains the same but that extra arrangements are made to provide for pupils with SEN.

If this distinction is accepted, inclusion is presented as aiming to encourage schools to reconsider their structure, teaching approaches, pupil grouping and use of support so that the school responds to the perceived needs of all its pupils. Teachers seek opportunities to look at new ways of involving all pupils and to draw on experimentation and reflection. Collaboration is important. There should be planned access to a broad and balanced curriculum developed from its foundations as a curriculum for all pupils. Although some take the view that inclusion is about getting more pupils in mainstream schools and fewer or none in special schools and other venues regarded as segregating, it may be argued that special schools can also be inclusive (Farrell 2000). The Qualifications and Curriculum Authority for example take the view that inclusion means 'securing appropriate opportunities for learning, assessment and qualifications to enable the full and effective participation of all pupils in the process of learning' (Wade 1999).

Three aspects of inclusion

Social inclusion

One aspect of inclusion is social inclusion which was the theme of two government circulars, 10/99 (DfEE 1999c) and 11/99 (DfEE 1999d).

Circular 10/99 highlights the need to provide for pupils in school rather than physically excluding them through short-term or permanent exclusions. Among ways of cutting down such exclusion from school is seeking to reduce disaffection in particular among pupils in known high-risk categories. Among these categories are pupils with SEN who may develop challenging behaviour and pupils whose attainments tend to be very low.

Approaches to such pupils include early intervention, careful planning, and whole school strategies. School-based pastoral support programmes (PSP) are developed with the help of external services for pupils who are at serious risk of permanent exclusion or of being drawn into criminal behaviour. For pupils who already have Individual Education Plans, these IEPs should be made to encompass the features of a PSP. Normally, a PSP will have been put into operation and will have failed before the school resorts to exclusion. Once a pupil is excluded, the head teachers and the LEA should plan for his or her reintegration into school-based education.

It will be seen that the guidance in *Circular 10/99* indicates groups of pupils who appear to be at risk of exclusion. The school had to be careful of course that in identifying such pupils they were not contributing to a self-fulfilling prophesy and expecting disaffection where there might be none. The Circular then suggested strategies to avoid exclusion and explained documentation that would indicate that the school had consulted outside specialists and had not been precipitous in excluding a pupil. Finally, it set expectations that plans would be made for pupils' reintegration.

Circular 11/99 concerned the LEA's role in supporting pupils at risk of exclusion or who had been excluded. It emphasises that pupils excluded for more than three weeks should get a suitable full-time alternative education. LEAs and other agencies should work to reduce exclusions in line with a national target. The LEA must consider compelling school attendance through legal remedies and should support schools that have pupils with PSPs.

It was noted as early as 1998 that pupils with statements of SEN are more likely to be excluded from school than other pupils (Donovan 1998). While this should receive attention, it should be noted how many pupils with statements who are excluded, have those statements because of behavioural, emotional and social difficulties. If the behaviour of these pupils is such that the school considers it can no longer properly educate them, it is this that should be the focus of attention, not the statements as such.

Having considered the two *Circulars*, the relationship between raising the standards of attainment of pupils with SEN and social inclusion should be evident. If the probability of school exclusion is increased when attainment is low, it may be that the better the attainment of a pupil with SEN (or other pupils), the less likely the prospect of exclusion. Also, as a strategy, social inclusion is likely to raise the standards attained by a pupil with SEN for the simple reason that a child is likely (though sadly not inevitably) to attain more when he is in school than when he is not being educated at all. So social inclusion in the sense used in these Circulars would appear to support the raising of standards of attainment for pupils with SEN (and other pupils). To provide an education for a pupil in a school or other educational establishment is likely to do more for his learning than his not having any formal education at all.

Including pupils with SEN already in mainstream school

A second thread of inclusion is that of including pupils with SEN who are already in mainstream schools. This approach seems to be the purpose of documents seeking to encourage this kind of inclusion such as the *Index for Inclusion* (Booth, Ainscow and Black-Hawkins 2000*)*. The document concerns the inclusion of all those connected with the school, adults as well as children, not only pupils with SEN.

It addresses three dimensions of schooling: creating inclusive cultures, producing inclusive policies, and evolving inclusive practices. Each dimension is exemplified by a number of indicators that may be used to assess the current situation as well as planning to be, in the Index's terms, more inclusive in the future.

Within the dimension 'Creating inclusive cultures' one aspect is 'building a community' which includes, for example, the indicators 'everyone is made to feel welcome' and 'staff and students treat one another with respect'. A second aspect is 'establishing inclusive values' which is reflected in such indicators as 'everyone shares a philosophy for inclusion', and 'staff seek to remove all barriers to learning and participation in the school'.

The dimension 'producing inclusive policies' includes an aspect 'developing a school for all' which has indicators such as 'all new staff are helped to settle into the school' and 'the school seeks to admit all students from its locality'. Another aspect, 'organising support for diversity', includes the indicators "special needs' policies are inclusion policies' and 'the *Code of Practice* is used to reduce the barriers to learning and participation of all students'.

Within the dimension 'evolving inclusive practices' is an aspect 'orchestrating learning', which has indicators such as 'lessons are responsive to student diversity' and 'lessons develop an understanding of difference'. Within the aspect 'mobilising resources', are indicators like 'school resources are distributed fairly to support inclusion' and 'student difference is used as a resource for teaching and learning'.

In general, including pupils already in mainstream school involves developing a culture in mainstream schools for inclusion, encouraging schools to review their structure, teaching approaches, pupil grouping and use of support to enable them to respond to the diverse learning needs of all pupils. Teachers would develop opportunities to consider new ways of involving pupils and employ experimentation and reflection. There would be planned access to a broad and balanced curriculum developed from its foundations as a curriculum for all pupils. Teachers will probably have values providing a rationale for inclusive practice, believing that pupils with SEN belong in mainstream classes. As well as a commitment to reviewing performance there will be a commitment to change. Teachers will draw on various teaching approaches. Collaborative problem solving will help teachers and others to seek solutions to challenges arising when teaching a diverse group of pupils.

To the extent that pupils with SEN are included in the school ethos and in lessons, it would be expected that they would be likely to learn more than if they were not included. As learning normally equates with better progress and attainment, it will be seen that improving the inclusion of a pupil in the appropriate learning environment will raise standards of attainment. Put another way, this approach to inclusion could be justified on the grounds of raising standards of attainment and achievement in school subjects and in personal, behavioural and social development.

Developing an inclusive ethos and inclusive approaches may increase the school's capacity to include pupils who are presently not in mainstream or who otherwise might be considered to be better placed in another setting such as a special school or a pupil referral unit. This leads to a consideration of the third aspect of inclusion, the balance of pupils in mainstream schools and other settings such as special schools.

Attempts to assess and encourage inclusion use local authority and commercially developed quality marks. For example, Medway Council has an 'Inclusive Schools Quality Mark' which is awarded to schools demonstrating inclusive practice. This involves looking at three aspects of school life:

• an inclusive ethos
• inclusive policies and
• inclusive practices.

For example, a school might be able to demonstrate that it is welcoming to a pupil with a disability. It will have a policy that describes how the pupil will be provided for. The school will have day-to-day practices to ensure that the pupil can move safely around school, have personal care needs taken care of and so on (www.medway.gov.uk/index/learning/inclusion/363.html).

The balance of pupils in mainstream and special schools

Increasing inclusion

As indicated above, inclusion may result in increasing the proportion of pupils in mainstream schools in relation to those in specialist provision such as that provided by a special school or a pupil referral unit. For some, including some so-called 'disability theorists', the appropriate 'balance' would be no balance at all. No pupils would be educated in special schools or other settings and all pupils with SEN would be educated in mainstream schools.

The expression 'full inclusion' as it applies to pupils with SEN indicates the view that all pupils with SEN should be educated in mainstream schools. A range of provision in which SEN could be met (such as mainstream school, special school, pupil referral unit, home tuition) would not be acceptable. It would be better to have increased support and resources in mainstream schools in proportion to the severity and complexity of SEN (e.g. Gartner and Lipsky 1989).

Full inclusion is not the policy of the Government nor is it that of any of the major parties in opposition at the time of writing.

The Green Paper

In October 1997, the Government published a Green Paper, a consultation document, on special education, *Excellence for All Children: Meeting Special Educational Needs* (DfEE 1997b). Although there have been important developments since the publication of this document, it is illuminating to remember the rather restricted view of inclusion that it presented and its concern with standards.

The publication claimed to concern standards, shifting resources to practical support and increasing inclusion. Building on views expressed in an earlier consultation document (Kilfoyle 1997) and signalled in the White Paper *Excellence in Schools* (DfEE 1997a), the Green Paper sought to set the future direction of special education.

Some confusion was evident even in the earlier Labour Party paper (Kilfoyle 1997) which used the terms 'inclusion' and 'integration' interchangeably. The Green Paper itself gave no explicit and coherent definition of inclusion such as can be found elsewhere (e.g. Clarke *et al.* 1995). Its view appears to be that inclusion applies only to children being educated in ordinary schools rather than special schools or elsewhere. This suggests that to place a pupil in a special school is to exclude. In line with this, the Green Paper sees the peers of pupils with SEN as children in mainstream schools. It states:

> The ultimate purpose of SEN provision is to enable young people to flourish in adult life. There are therefore strong educational, as well as social and moral, grounds for educating children with SEN with

their peers. We aim to increase the level and quality of inclusion within mainstream schools, while protecting and enhancing specialist provision for those who need it.

(DfEE 1997b, p. 43)

What exactly the 'strong educational as well as social and moral grounds for educating children with SEN with their peers' are, is not explained. Nevertheless, the Green Paper envisages the continuation of special schools, stating that 'parents will continue to have a right to express a preference for a special school' (Ch. 4, para. 4).

The Green Paper, as has been indicated, was a consultation document and in this sense has been superseded by other developments represented in other documents. It is to these that we now turn.

Removing Barriers to Achievement

THE DOCUMENT IN OUTLINE

A document, *Removing Barriers to Achievement: The Government's Strategy for SEN* (Department for Education and Employment 2004b), sets out a timetable for 2004–5 for implementing various policies. Mention is made of *Every Child Matters* (Department for Education and Skills 2003) (purchasable from www.tso.co.uk/bookshop). This signalled changes in children's services focusing on early intervention, preventative work and integrated services for children through 'Children's Trusts'.

Removing Barriers itself aims to:

- personalise learning for all children
- make education more innovative and responsive to the diverse needs of individual children
- (related to point 2) reduce the reliance on separate SEN structures and process
- raise the achievement of children considered to have SEN.

(paraphrased from DfES 2004b, p. 7)

The document concerns: early intervention; removing barriers to learning; raising expectations and achievement; and delivering improvements in partnership.

Concerning early intervention, the aim is to ensure that pupils with SEN get the 'help they need' (ibid., p. 8) as soon as possible and that their parents have access to suitable childcare. This includes having health, education and social care 'organised around the needs of children and their families' (ibid., p. 10).

It is anticipated that barriers to learning might be removed through 'inclusive practice' (ibid., p. 8). The government wants to see 'schools with the confidence to innovate' and 'schools working together to support the inclusion of all children from their local community' (ibid., p. 26).

The focus of raising expectations and achievement is developing teachers' skills and strategies for 'meeting the needs of children with SEN' and focusing better on 'the progress that children make' (ibid., p. 8).

Delivering improvements in partnership would involve 'taking a hands-on approach to improvement so that parents can be confident that their child will get the education they need' (ibid., p. 8).

IMPROVING THE ACHIEVEMENT OF PUPILS WITH SEN

Among the strengths of *Removing Barriers to Achievement* is its acknowledgement in certain sections of the importance of pupils' progress and achievement. The Government wants to see 'improved data giving parents and teachers a clearer picture of how well children working below age-related expectations are progressing' (ibid., p. 50). It proposes to 'deliver practical teaching and learning resources to raise the achievement of children with SEN through the Primary Strategy and strengthen the focus in Key Stage 3 on young people with SEN who are falling behind their peers' (ibid., p. 50). Also, the Government (referring to the National Curriculum) intends to 'promote and extend the use of P scales to measure the progress of pupils working below level 1 and collect this data nationally from 2005' (ibid., p. 51). It will 'consult on changes to the performance tables so that schools get credit for the achievements of all pupils, including those with SEN' (ibid., p. 51).

SOME CONFUSIONS IN THE DOCUMENT

Removing Barriers seems confused about the pupils to whom it applies. The sub-title of the document is 'The Government's Strategy for SEN', but the foreword by the Secretary of State for Education and Skills refers to children with 'special educational needs and disabilities' (DfES 2003, p. 3). It is not clear whether this is those children with disabilities who do not have SEN or children with disabilities that do have SEN. The forward includes comments by the Minister for Disabled People writing of 'young people with learning difficulties and disabilities' (ibid., p. 5). It is unclear whether these young people have 'learning difficulties' related to 'difficulty in learning' or 'disability', why these 'learning difficulties' should be assumed to equate with SEN and again whether one is considering 'disability' that does or does not constitute a SEN. Where such confusion in terminology is repeated in the document, it is unclear to which children it is referring.

Further vagueness with expressions arises with terms such as 'potential', 'needs' and 'inclusive practice' to which it is very difficult to attach meaning. For example, children should be reaching their 'full potential' (ibid., p. 6) and the Government wants teachers to have the skills and confidence 'to help children with SEN to reach their potential' (ibid., p. 50). Yet how this potential can be identified and how it would be known whether or not a child had reached its full potential is not made clear. There are ways in which the notion of potential could be more precise if it was more securely related to notions of benchmarking and added value but the document does not make this link.

We are told that 'too many children wait too long to have their needs met' (ibid., p. 7). The whole thorny issue about what these needs are and how it can be known if and when they are met is not tackled.

Again, it is claimed that the Government will 'help schools to develop effective inclusive practice' (ibid., p. 27) and will ensure that leadership programmes 'promote inclusive practice', but it is not made clear what 'inclusive practice' is.

Where both 'needs' and 'inclusive practice' are brought together, the meaning is more evasive, as when the Government explains that 'To help schools become more effective at responding to the needs of individual pupils, we will launch a new Inclusion Development Programme' (ibid., p. 31).

Readers will not be surprised, if, in line with the theme of this book, it is suggested that some of the fog of this confusion would be lifted if standards of pupils' attainment and achievement were brought to bear. 'Potential' might then be related to judgement about what other pupils with similar types of SEN achieve in terms of expected progress with reference to target-setting and benchmarking (see the case study at the end of this chapter for how such judgements are made). 'Needs' would be related to (or replaced by) a consideration of the type of SEN and what works to improve progress and attainment. 'Inclusion' would be understood in terms of 'optimal education' (see below p. 101).

Inclusive Schooling

The Education Act 1993 section 160 (later consolidated into the Education Act 1996 section 316) set out for the first time the principle that a child with SEN should, where this was what parents wanted, normally be educated at a mainstream school. There were three conditions, all of which had to be satisfied before mainstream provision was considered appropriate. These were:

- The mainstream provision had to be able to ensure that the child received the educational provision his or her learning difficulty called for.
- It had to be ensured that others with whom the child with SEN was being educated received effective education.
- Resources had to be used efficiently.

The document *Inclusive Schooling: Children with Special Educational Needs* (DfES 2001b) gives statutory guidance on the framework for inclusion within the Education Act 1996. The Special Educational Needs and Disability Act 2001 is said to deliver a 'strengthened right to a mainstream education for children with special educational needs' (ibid., p. 1, paragraph 4) by amending the Education Act 1996.

This section concentrates on two aspects of the document. The first concerns the interface of this 'right' with the 'right' of parents to express a preference for a school for their child. The second is the constrained nature of the right to inclusion apparent in the document.

Turning to the first issue, there is a lack of even-handedness in the recommended response to parents expressing a preference for either a mainstream or special school for their child. It is stated that:

> The Act seeks to enable more children who have special educational needs to be included successfully within mainstream education. This clearly signals that where parents want a mainstream education for their child everything possible should be done to provide it. Equally where parents want a special school place their wishes should be listened to and taken into account.
>
> (ibid., 1.4)

It is not clear why the response to a parent wanting a mainstream school for their child is that 'everything possible should be done to provide it', while for a parent wanting a special school 'their wishes should be listened to and taken into account'. The contrast between these two responses is made all the more noticeable by the use of the word 'equally' when what is being stated is not an equal response at all. Also a parent expressing a preference for a mainstream school has 'wants' while a parent expressing a preference for a special school has 'wishes'.

Concerning the second issue, that of the nature of the proposed 'right' to inclusion, it is clear that this is constrained. If one is not careful, the use of the word 'right' can appear to imply an absolute right to do something or to demand something. The 'right' to life is of this sort. What is proposed in the document is not such a right. There was no absolute right to mainstream education before the Special Educational Needs and Disability Act 2001 and there is no absolute right to mainstream education after it. This is indicated by the *Inclusive Schooling* document referring to a 'strengthened right' to mainstream education (ibid., 1.4). The right (if that is the correct word) is partial.

The extent of the right can be seen from the commensurate duties that are placed on others in connection with the 'right'.

THE RIGHT TO BE EDUCATED IN THE MAINSTREAM

As a result of the Special Educational Needs and Disability Act 2001, the Education Act 1996 section 316(3) was amended to read:

> If a statement is maintained under section 324 for the child, he must be educated in a mainstream school unless that is incompatible with:
> a) the wishes of his parent, or
> b) the provision of efficient education for other children.

The use of the word, 'must' in the above section of the Act indicates the duty of the LEA and others that correspond to the 'right' to be educated in the mainstream. If the education of a child with SEN is incompatible with the efficient education of other pupils, mainstream education can only be refused if there are no reasonable steps that can be taken to prevent the incompatibility. But it may not be possible to take steps to prevent a child's inclusion being incompatible with the efficient education of others. This may arise for example when a child's behaviour systematically, persistently and significantly threatens the safety or impedes the learning of others. It may also arise where the teacher, even with other support, has to spend a greatly disproportionate amount of time with the child in relation to the rest of the class.

The 'rights' are further affected when one considers a particular school rather than the generic concept of 'mainstream'. A parent may want mainstream provision for their child who has SEN, and may express a preference for a particular mainstream school to be named in their child's statement. In this case, schedule 27 of the Education Act 1996 requires the LEA to name the parents' preferred choice of school in the child's statement unless any of three conditions are not met. These conditions are:

- the school cannot provide for the needs of the child
- the child's inclusion at the school would be incompatible with the efficient education of other pupils
- the child's inclusion at the school would be incompatible with the efficient use of resources.

It will be seen that there is still no comprehensive 'right' of attendance at a mainstream school, but that the rights of the parents of a child with SEN are balanced against the 'rights' of the parents of children who do not have SEN and against other factors.

How standards of attainment and achievement can inform decisions about the balance of pupils in mainstream and special schools

If the above summary is correct, it will be seen that several points arise. Full inclusion is not on the table for the present government or any government in waiting, nor is there any suggestion that it will be in the foreseeable future. The Green Paper was concerned not just with inclusion but also with raising standards of pupils' attainment and achievement. The programme for action continues this theme. Although the document *Inclusive Schooling: Children with Special Educational Needs* (DfES 2001b) indicates an equivocal approach to the preferences of parents with regard to mainstream or special school, there is no comprehensive 'right' of inclusion in mainstream school.

Given the above, any approach to the balance of pupils attending mainstream or special schools has to be informed by parental preference. I suggest that an important consideration is also the standards of attainment and achievement reached by pupils in different settings. I previously outlined this approach (Farrell 2000) calling it 'educational inclusion'. As this term is easy to confuse with any approach to including more pupils with SEN in mainstream school whether this is informed by standards or not, I propose that a better name for the approach is 'optimal education'.

In what follows therefore, I wish to examine an approach called, 'optimal education' and how:

- optimal education is more informed than is usual by the standards of achievement and attainment reached by pupils with SEN
- optimal education can inform the proportion of time spent in mainstream and special school
- optimal education avoids demeaning children attending special schools and staff working in them
- optimal education can lead to the improvement of the capacity of mainstream schools to effectively include more pupils with SEN
- optimal inclusion can be related to parental preference of school.

In optimal education, a key part in deciding whether mainstream provision is appropriate, is that it should result in raising the pupils' standards of attainment and achievement in the broadest sense indicated in earlier chapters. Given a choice between a special school and a mainstream school, the benefit of the doubt would be given to the mainstream school, as the special school would be able to demonstrate that it raises standards better than a mainstream school for pupils with particular types of SEN. Such a judgement would also inform the proportion of time that a pupil is educated in mainstream and special school, for example where a mainstream and a special school were located on the same campus (co-located in the current jargon).

Given that there is a continuing role for special schools (unsurprisingly as in England around 100,000 pupils continue to attend them), optimal education seeks to avoid the implication that special schools are inferior to mainstream schools. The Green Paper did not reveal what it thought were the educational, social and moral reasons why pupils should be educated in a mainstream school. By contrast, optimal education argues and presents evidence in support of the view that there are educational, social and moral grounds for educating pupils in special schools, namely that a good special school can raise standards of attainment and achievement in personal, social, behavioural and cognitive development of pupils with SEN.

This does not preclude of course a mainstream school improving its curriculum, assessment, organisation, ethos and other features to try to reach the same or better standards for pupils with SEN than local special schools. Where this happens, then mainstream placement could be justified in optimal education terms. This may involve looking at different rates of progress and attainment for pupils with different types of SEN. For example, a mainstream school might be able to perform as well for pupils with moderate learning difficulties as a local special school but not as well with pupils having severe behavioural, emotional and social difficulties.

Parental preference for a special school or a mainstream school and optimal education can be combined. Data is used relating to the relative progress and standards of pupils with similar types of SEN and starting from comparable levels as indicated by baseline assessment. This data is made available to parents, schools and others to inform, should parents wish to consider it, their decision about an appropriate school for their child.

Case study 4: Hampshire LEA: informing parental preference for mainstream or special school

The following case study illustrates how data on standards is collected and collated by one LEA, Hampshire, so that, among other things, it can inform judgements about placements and parental preference in mainstream or special schools.

Hampshire LEA uses a system of collecting data and using mathematical modelling. The data relates to the P scales and National Curriculum levels. Data is collected annually for:

- pupils with a statement of SEN attending mainstream schools with special resourced provision/units
- pupils attending special schools
- many pupils attending primary schools and having statements of SEN.

The LEA has provided exemplars across the subjects for P scales 1 through 8. It is developing approaches to moderate judgements of teachers about P levels to help ensure consistency and reliability. The LEA collates the data on attainment and progress and has done so since the year 2000 to produce mathematically modelled 'trend lines' for pupils in the county. Comparisons can therefore be made of the progress that pupils with SEN make in mainstream and special schools.

Also, the progress data has been published since 2003 in a standardised way, allowing schools to see how a particular pupil has progressed in relation to an average child of the same age with the same type of SEN. A school can also see whether, for example, its pupils at Key Stage 1 with SEN progressed further in, say, numeracy than was typical across the county.

At present this data is available for pupils with severe learning difficulties and moderate learning difficulties. It has not been viable to extend the approach to other types of SEN such as behavioural, emotional and social difficulties or to communication difficulties such as autism and speech and language difficulties. This is because:

- wide discrepancies in the performance level of pupils make any trends difficult to determine; or,
- the small number of pupils on which the analysis would be based would limit the accuracy of statistical inferences.

For each type of SEN, trends are indicated for sub-sections of the P scales:

- personal, social and health education (PSHE) (attention, independent organisational skills)
- mathematics (shape, space and measure; using and applying)
- English (reading, writing, speaking and listening).

For each area of SEN, for example, for moderate learning difficulties, trend lines are produced for pupils scoring at a level at which:

- only the lowest 5 per cent score
- only the lowest 25 per cent score
- 50 per cent of pupils score
- only the highest 25 per cent score
- only the highest 5 per cent score.

The trend lines indicate the attainment of pupils aged four to 18 years.

There are various ways of using the data. One way is to identify an individual pupil's starting point in a specified year, for example

P scale level 2 in the reception year, and then to determine the trend line of best fit. This can then be used as a basis for setting subsequent targets and for judging the value added above the county trend. This judgement can be made for individual pupils or for groups of pupils as to whether they attend special school or mainstream school. The data can be analysed in different ways to consider the progress of pupils of different groups, for example boys and girls or groups of pupils with different ethnic backgrounds.

Importantly, the data can be analysed to judge the relative progress of pupils in mainstream and in special schools. This allows the LEA, schools, parents and others to make judgements based on evidence of progress about the cost–benefits of the inclusion of pupils in mainstream schools.

(Based on information kindly supplied by Hampshire LEA)

Summary/conclusion

In this chapter, I distinguished between integration and inclusion. I outlined social inclusion, the inclusion of pupils already in mainstream schools, and the balance of pupils with SEN in mainstream and special schools. In relation to the balance of pupils in mainstream and special schools, the chapter argued for 'optimal inclusion', taking into account the standards of pupils' attainment reached in whatever venue provides the pupil's education. This may be solely or predominantly a mainstream school, a special school, a pupil referral unit or another venue. A case study illustrated the use of information on the attainment and progress of pupils with SEN to inform judgements concerning inclusion of pupils in mainstream schools.

Thinking points

Readers may wish to consider:

• the pros and cons of 'optimal education' that uses evidence of pupils' attainment and progress.

Key texts

Department for Education and Employment (2004b) *Removing Barriers to Achievement: The Government's Strategy for SEN,* London: DfEE

As indicated, this sets out a timetable for 2004–5 for what the Government perceives as removing barriers.

Department for Education and Skills (2001b) *Inclusive Schooling: Children with Special Educational Needs,* London: DfES

Readers should note the difficulty that the document finds in trying to balance supposed rights for parents to express a preference for a special or a mainstream school and the apparent intention to increase the inclusion of pupils with SEN in mainstream school.

Chapter 7

Special educational funding according to achievement

Introduction

There is no doubting the importance of funding and its equitable distribution in education and specifically in relation to SEN. Potential lack of agreement about what SEN is, what types of SEN are and whether 'needs' are being met, add to the challenge of devising equitable approaches.

This chapter explains the national and local arrangements for allocating resources for SEN in England. Within this context, the chapter then outlines recent government guidance on SEN expenditure and its relation to the attainment of pupils and comments upon selected chapters and sections of the guidance. I have separated the government guidance and my own suggestions under the headings 'guidance' and 'comments'. A case study describes the work of a particular local education authority, indicating how aspects of this guidance can be seen in a particular funding system.

National allocation of funds in England

In England, the Department for Education and Skills indicates what it expects individual LEAs to spend based on a national formula called the Formula Spending Share. This distributes in a notional way the available funding to all LEAs. In practice, each local authority spends at a level determined by its councillors (locally elected politicians). This is broadly funded from:

- council tax (a local tax for local services)
- national non-domestic rates (a pooled national business rate where local authorities are entitled to an amount per head of population rather than a share of what they have in fact collected), and

- revenue support grant (directed funding for local authorities from central government).

Principally, the funding is distributed on the basis of pupil numbers, but there are other factors relating to different costs of living in different regions, population sparseness and additional educational needs (AEN). The AEN element is predominantly based on indices of social deprivation:

- pupils with English as an additional language
- parents of working families on tax credit
- parents on income support
- low-achieving ethnic groups.

Another category of 'need' for high-cost pupils uses the proportion of the population on income support and low birth weight as indicators of need.

The approach to allocating funds described above might suggest that the DfES is drawing strong parallels between social deprivation and SEN. However, across LEAs there may be no reason to adjust for SEN because it is likely that pupils with the most severe SEN are evenly distributed across England. These are the roughly three per cent of pupils that have a statement of SEN. However, this view does not imply that schools will in fact have a uniform distribution of such pupils.

The fact that different LEAs have substantially different proportions of pupils with statements of SEN does not disprove this theory. Instead, it may highlight different local practices, most importantly the point at which an individual pupil's SEN triggers the statutory assessment process that may lead to a statement of SEN being issued. The DfES has avoided the use of subjective data in the Formula Spending Shares, recognising that it can produce perverse incentives.

Local allocation of funds in England

Funds not normally delegated to mainstream schools

In England, LEA expenditure on SEN covers a range of factors. Costs *not* normally delegated to mainstream schools include those relating to:

- educational psychologists
- Special support services staff who work with pupils at the 'Early Years Action Plus' and the 'School Action Plus' aspect of the *Special Educational Needs Code of Practice* (DfES 2001a); that is,

pupils for whom extra support is required from outside the school but not a statement of SEN

- educational welfare officers (although their work covers other pupils not having SEN)
- 'out of borough' pupils; that is, pupils who attend schools outside the funding LEA such as day or residential special schools
- pupils who attend the LEA's own special schools
- units and support for pupils excluded from schools (although not all these pupils have SEN)
- administration costs such as those for the writing and maintaining of statements of SEN
- transport for pupils with SEN.

With regard to such services as educational psychologists, SEN support services staff and education welfare officers, there is often discussion about the time allocated to different schools. This may reflect the number of pupils with SEN in a school, but there are of course other aspects of the work of these support staff. Nevertheless, these centrally funded services are used more by some schools than others and therefore the funds used on these services are allocated in different ways to different schools.

Funds normally delegated to mainstream schools

Funds normally delegated to mainstream schools may comprise:

- non-specific funds for SEN allocated according to a formula based on the number of pupils and their type of SEN
- funds allocated through a proxy indicator, such as pupil eligibility for free school meals
- funds allocated according to an audit of SEN or by some other means.

Some funds are allocated according to a formula based on the number of pupils and their age. This is sometimes called the 'age weighted pupil unit', or AWPU. This element of formula funding is opaque and it is not possible to point to the particular component of the AWPU and demonstrate that it is the element for SEN. The AWPU argument is based on the principle that the basic level of funding received by schools ought to be sufficient to meet the needs of pupils within a reasonable range. It assumes that this can be done without the school needing additional support for pupils with SEN whether with or without statements. The funding is also seen to support the costs of SEN co-ordinators which are required in all schools regardless of the number of pupils with SEN.

Some funds may be distributed by the LEA to local schools via a formula that depends on the 'levels' of SEN in each school related to the *Code* (DfES 2001a).

Government guidance in relation to the attainment of pupils with SEN

The remaining sections of this chapter consider the government guidance, *The Management of SEN Expenditure* (DfES 2004a), to the extent that it relates to the attainment and achievement of pupils with SEN. The guidance comprises the following chapters and sections

---

Introduction
1   **Delegating Resources to Mainstream Settings**
2   **Monitoring and Accountability**
3   **Independent and Non-Maintained Special Schools**
4   **Maintained Special Schools and Additionally Resourced Provision**
5   Managing Change
6   Reporting on Expenditure Through Section 52
      Detailed Information
a)   **Meeting Statutory Requirements**
b)   Resources for SEN in Early Years Settings
c)   Resources for Post-16 SEN in the Schools Sector
d)   Examples of Successful Practice

Selected chapters and sections of the guidance picked out in bold in the above panel are examined and commented on below.

The Introduction

The guidance

The guidance maintains that there are concerns about above-inflation increases in local authority expenditure on SEN. An investigation into SEN expenditure indicated that:

- local authorities that have worked with schools to increase the dele-
  gation of SEN resources have been more successful in containing
  increases in centrally managed budgets
- many local authorities do not yet have adequate arrangements for
  monitoring outcomes for pupils with SEN, especially in relation to
  funding delegated to schools
- there was a need for more consistency and transparent reporting of
  expenditure on SEN between local authorities (DfES 2004a, pp.
  7–8). (See also www.teachernet.gov.uk/sen.)

Comments

The guidance provides information and suggested approaches for LEAs
to manage SEN expenditure. To some extent it relates to the attainment
and achievement of pupils with SEN.

Delegating resources to mainstream settings

The guidance

With regard to delegating resources to mainstream settings, the
Government recommends that local arrangements should, among other
things, support raising 'standards of achievement' and match the allocation of resources with responsibility for 'outcomes in terms of pupil
progress, attainment and well being'. At the same time local arrangements should 'support early intervention and inclusive practice' and
'support inclusion within mainstream schools wherever possible' (DfES
2004a, p. 10).

The guidance suggests that resource allocations might be understood
in three ways. Firstly, there are those provided through a formula for
pupils with moderate 'needs'. These are additional educational needs
(AEN) and some SEN. Secondly, there are resources that are provided on
an ongoing basis for predictable groups of pupils with 'severe and complex' SEN. An example might be special resourced provision in a
mainstream school. Thirdly, there are resources provided for pupils with
'complex and enduring' SEN on an individual basis (DfES 2004a, p. 11).
Local authorities should develop a funding formula to allocate resources
for most pupils with AEN and SEN. Among indicators used by LEAs to
calculate AEN/SEN formula allocations are 'prior attainment based
upon end of Key Stage test data', 'reading test scores', 'cognitive ability
indicators' and other factors (DfES 2004a, pp. 11–12).

Local authorities should develop arrangements to distribute 'additional resources' for pupils with the most severe and complex SEN. The guidance suggests certain steps for this including developing 'clear criteria' for the allocation of top-up resources in partnership with schools. The local authority should 'agree a partnership arrangement with head teachers to manage the allocations' and this could be a panel on a cluster or an area basis (DfES 2004a, p. 12). Local authorities should ensure that resources are allocated on various bases: 'evidence of need', 'progress' and 'provision required to address barriers to learning' (DfES 2004a, p. 12).

Comments

The recognition of the importance of attainment and achievement of pupils with SEN is welcome, but there are areas of unresolved tension and vagueness in the document.

Local arrangements are supposed to support raising 'standards of achievement' and match the allocation of resources with responsibility for 'outcomes in terms of pupil progress, attainment and well being', and at the same time 'support early intervention and inclusive practice' and 'support inclusion within mainstream schools wherever possible' (DfES 2004a p. 10).

The tensions between raising attainment and achievement and inclusion in mainstream schools 'wherever possible' are not sufficiently examined. For example, it is clearly *possible* to 'include' all children with SEN including those presently in special schools, in additionally resourced provision (such as units) and in pupil referral units in the sense of physically teaching these pupils in a mainstream classroom. The question is whether it is justifiable and whether it would provide a better education for pupils with SEN and other pupils.

There is vagueness in the exhortation that authorities should ensure that resources are allocated on various bases: 'evidence of need', 'progress' and 'provision required to address barriers to learning' (DfES 2004a, p. 12). Of these the most useful focus is perhaps 'progress' as this can be defined. The term 'need' is a bit vague (see Farrell 2004b, pp. 11–25 for a discussion of problems concerning goal-related and unconditional need). It is not clear what 'required' suggests in relation to provision and what 'address' means in relation to supposed 'barriers' to learning.

Monitoring and accountability

The guidance

Regarding monitoring and accountability, the guidance recommends that all local authorities 'develop systematic accountability arrangements' and that these are based on 'school self-review and focus on pupil outcomes and thresholds for support and challenge' (DfES 2004a, p. 15). The focus on pupil outcomes involves 'scrutinising the achievements and progress of different groups of pupils, including those working below age related expectations' (DfES 2004a, p. 16). The guidance recommends that LEAs provide schools with a budget statement indicating how AEN and SEN resources are allocated. LEAs could provide a planning tool to help schools link resources to the school's provision for groups of pupils and individuals so that the school can 'evaluate their use of resources in relation to pupils' progress and attainment' (DfES 2004a, p. 18).

Some local authorities are said to have been very effective in 'promoting inclusive education, in developing the role of special schools and in managing cost of "out of authority" placements whilst maintaining the quality of provision' (DfES 2004a, p. 7).

School assessment and performance data can help in this respect. Annual performance data profiles in the form of the Pupil Achievement Tracker (PAT) allow schools to enter additional voluntary assessments. The DfES hopes to add a facility to 'record achievement below test levels' (DfES 2004a, p. 18). The PAT can produce value-added trend lines to show the respective progress made by groups and individuals. The guidance suggests that LEAs may wish to provide schools with 'additional performance indicators regarding inclusion'. Some of these could be used as 'filters' within the PAT to 'focus on individuals or groups of learners and evaluate the impact of particular interventions on progress' (DfES 2004a, p. 18). The DfES intends to collect (from 2005) P level attainment data as part of the national data collection exercise and adds this to the PAT performance profile. For further information on P scales see www.nc.uk.net/Id.

Any local scheme, according to the guidance, should among other things be based on agreed outcome measures enabling the school to 'compare the effectiveness of its provision for pupils with SEN to that achieved by similar schools' (ibid., p. 19). Outcome measures should include those related to 'pupil attainment, social and emotional development and social inclusion, and achievement in its wider sense' (ibid., p. 19). Parents should have clear information about, 'the progress and attainments of their child' (ibid., p. 20).

Comments

Again the attention to attainment and achievement is encouraging but there is also vagueness about what, 'quality of provision' might mean and the extent to which attainment and achievement are part of this.

Local authorities should 'develop systematic accountability arrangements' based on 'school self-review and focus on pupil outcomes and thresholds for support and challenge' (DfES 2004a, p. 15). The focus on pupil outcomes involves 'scrutinising the achievements and progress of different groups of pupils, including those working below age related expectations …' (DfES 2004a, p. 16). As indicated in other chapters of the present book 'pupil outcomes' can include attainment and achievement in many areas including personal and social development.

The guidance states that some local authorities have been very effective in 'promoting inclusive education, in developing the role of special schools and in managing cost of out of authority placements whilst maintaining the quality of provision' (DfES 2004a, p. 7). This is particularly vague. It is important if such statements are to mean anything that such notions as 'quality of provision' are made clear. If such quality refers to the standards of attainment of pupils with SEN and if this has been successfully maintained and improved while the other features have been pursued, this needs to be made explicit. It needs to be made clear that standards of attainment of pupils with SEN have risen or been maintained, if, for example, local authorities have been reducing the number of pupils in special schools and reducing the number of pupils in out of authority special schools.

Independent and non-maintained special schools

The guidance

With regard to independent and non-maintained special schools, the guidance recommends that education authorities 'review each placement and consider pupil progress and possible arrangements for reintegration to a more local environment' (ibid., p. 28).

Comments

Again the potential tension between the progress of the pupil and his or her reintegration (or inclusion) in the local environment will be noted.

Maintained special schools and additionally resourced provision

The guidance

There is an emphasis on arrangements to support special 'outreach' and 'temporary, part-time and dual registered placements' (ibid., p. 30).

Comments

When the guidance comes to consider maintained special schools and additionally resourced provision, there is little mention of standards of pupils' attainment.

Meeting statutory requirements

The guidance

The section of the guidance headed 'meeting statutory assessments' is concerned with statements of SEN and related matters.

The guidance notes that 'Where statements are maintained, LAs, in partnership with schools, must ensure that required provision can be delivered. Most resources may be distributed on a whole school basis but there must be arrangements in place to ensure that provision is made even where the relevant budget is delegated' (ibid., p. 40, section A).

Comments

About three per cent of pupils in England have a statement of SEN. The LEA is responsible for identifying the needs of pupils with SEN who require a statement and for providing the additional resources that are required to meet their needs. The statement provides the legal entitlement for the pupil to receive the provision it outlines, while the LEA has the legal responsibility to ensure that the provision specified in the statement is made.

While the funding may be delegated to schools, the LEA still has the legal responsibility to ensure that the requirements of the statement are fulfilled. These requirements may take the form of extra equipment, additional support, specialist teaching or therapy such as speech and language therapy, where the therapist concerned may be employed not by the LEA but by the local health authority.

Costs to the LEA include those of producing and maintaining the statement. Potential costs also arise if a parent appeals against decisions of the LEA relating to the specification in a statement of school placement or the provision. Where the Special Educational Needs and Disability Tribunal (SENDIST) hears cases the LEA has to meet the costs of preparing a defence, travel for staff, opportunity costs for the use of staff time and the cost of making arrangements determined by the Tribunal.

Where a pupil is identified as requiring a statement of SEN attracting extra funding, there is a disincentive for schools and parents to have such funding terminated by having the statement rescinded. Some LEAs have developed so-called exit criteria. These are usually indications of a level of learning difficulty lower than that which suggested that a statement was necessary.

For example, a statement might be issued for a child aged 12 years old who had a reading age as indicated on a specified test of seven years. If, by the time the child was 13 years old, his reading age was eight years, then this might be agreed to be the point at which the statement was withdrawn and the child, for example, placed on the 'school support plus' point of the SEN framework.

These exit strategies assume that once a pupil has reached a level of attainment a little higher than the level that precipitated the statement, it would be appropriate to consider rescinding the statement and reducing support to lower level. Where the statement is related to a disability leading to a learning difficulty calling for special educational provision, the LEA would consider rescinding the statement for example when and if the degree of disability is reduced so that there is no longer a related learning difficulty.

Case study 5: Funding for SEN in Norfolk LEA

This case study outlines the system of funding in Norfolk LEA which reflects many of the approaches set out in the present chapter. Norfolk has a single system of formula funding for SEN whether it is non-statutory or involving pupils with statements of SEN. Like many LEAs, it is regularly reviewing its approaches and refining them as necessary. The case study focuses on funding for:

- pupils with statements of SEN
- pupils without statements
- schools with units for pupils with SEN
- schools with high levels of social deprivation, and
- special schools.

Pupils with statements of SEN

There are funding bands A to E with A representing the lowest funded band and E representing the highest. Pupils who are assessed and deemed to have very high levels of SEN are placed on funding band E. Funds for pupils in this band are allocated according to the level of provision required.

The assessment includes curriculum, behavioural, physical and medical care 'needs'. Curriculum needs are determined through the use of standardised tests of reading and mathematics for children other than those in the reception year. For reception children, the Bury Infant Check is used. If statutory aged pupils score below a specified level on the standardised tests, or if they have been assessed by professionals as having SEN, they are assessed further. For primary aged children, a curriculum checklist is used, while for secondary aged students, a diagnostic curriculum test is employed.

Pupils without statements of SEN

Pupils without statements of SEN are assessed on the same basis as those having statements. Funding bands are attributed according to scores in each of the assessed areas. The scores are calibrated (and re-calibrated as necessary) each year to make sure that the funds distributed equal the funds that are available. The assessment of curriculum, behavioural, physical and medical care 'needs' determines whether pupils are placed on bands A, B, C or D. Each band carries a level of funding which is given to the school to provide 'whole school' funding (not pupil-specific funding).

A percentage of SEN funding is distributed to all schools according to the three-year average of the number of pupils tested who score just below the threshold of band A (the lowest funded band). This is done through a so-called 'block allocation'. For each pupil in this category, the school receives a fixed sum which is also intended as whole school funding.

Schools with units for pupils with SEN

If a school has a unit for pupils with SEN, these are funded according to the number of pupils in them at any particular time, in other words, the funding is place-led. Additionally, the units receive fixed funds and may receive funding for notional pupils, depending on the numbers on roll. Also, because pupils are on the roll of the mainstream school of which the unit is a part, the school receives the appropriate age-weighted pupil allowance.

Schools with high levels of social deprivation

Schools having high levels of deprivation are provided with additional funds in line with three-year average levels of entitlement to free school meals at the school concerned.

Special schools

In special schools, pupil places are allocated according to five levels, according to the school profile indicated in the annual audit. This audit looks at curriculum need, care needs and behavioural needs. For each pupil, there is also an allocation of funds independent of the level of 'need'. Special schools with high levels of deprivation receive further funds. Finally, each school is allocated a fixed sum to help ensure that the range and balance of the curriculum is protected.

(Based on information kindly supplied by Norfolk LEA)

Summary/conclusion

This chapter explained the national and local arrangements for targeting resources for SEN in England, outlined recent government guidance on SEN expenditure and commented particularly on its relation to the attainment of pupils.

Thinking points

LEA officers (and school staff and parents wishing to encourage LEAs) may wish to consider:

*   the benefits of relating funding in part to the attainment of pupils with SEN

- how the allocation of funds for SEN can be best and most transparently explained and demonstrated to schools, parents and others.

Key text

Department for Education and Skills (2004) *The Management of SEN Expenditure,* London: DfES

This guidance, supplemented by a website, gives information and suggested approaches for LEAs to manage SEN expenditure.

Chapter 8

Using pupil attainment data for pupils with SEN and other information

Introduction

This chapter examines how data on the attainment and progress of pupils with SEN can be informed by other information about the pupils, namely gender, ethnicity, main learning difficulty, social background and age. A case study indicates how data on pupils with SEN may be used to inform and monitor the effectiveness of particular interventions.

Data on standards and progress

The data that is the concern of this chapter is to do with the attainment and progress of pupils with SEN in cognitive, behavioural, social and emotional development. It can involve assessments of literacy, numeracy, speech and language development, attainment in school subjects, assessments of behaviour, self-esteem and so on. I will use the example of reading attainment and progress.

Table 8.1 on the next page shows reading scores in terms of reading 'ages' for a group of fictitious pupils with SEN. In reality, the school would probably have data on more pupils but the figures below are simply for illustration.

It will be seen that the school has gathered assessments of reading for pupils identified as having SEN in a school. Repeating the assessment after a period of (in the example) six months, a second set of scores is obtained for the same pupils. By deducting the second score from the first, an indication of progress in months of reading is obtained for each pupil.

Next, a broad indication of the attainment of the pupils is obtained by adding the initial reading scores and dividing them by the number of pupils to give an average score. The second reading scores for each pupil are added and divided by the number of pupils to give the average scores

Table 8.1 Reading scores on two occasions in years and months for pupils aged 15 years

Pupil's name	January	June	Progress in months
David (B)	6 years, 7 months	7 years, 1 month	6 months
Anne (G)	7 years, 2 months	7 years, 6 months	4 months
Leanne (G)	5 years, 4 months	5 years, 5 months	1 month
Poojah (G)	7 years, 5 months	7 years, 10 months	5 months
Francine (G)	6 years, 4 months	6 years, 8 months	4 months
Nadim (B)	6 years, 6 months	6 years, 9 months	3 months
Javid (B)	5 years, 6 months	5 years, 11 months	5 months
Rocchina (G)	7 years, 3 months	7 years, 10 months	7 months
Michael (B)	6 years, 4 months	6 years, 8 months	4 months
Adam (B)	6 years, 2 months	6 years, 5 months	3 months

for the second testing. The second average score is deducted from the first average score to give the average progress (or the differences for each child are added and divided by the number of pupils). Looking at this average progress, the teachers will be able to see the individual pupils that have progressed less than or more than the average for the group. The teacher's knowledge of the pupils will inform judgements about whether the progress can be considered sufficient. If the points made in the earlier chapter on target-setting are remembered, the progress of each pupil might be compared with the target set for each, but this is not the focus of the present chapter.

Other factors that may have a bearing on progress

Having initially examined the data, one can consider factors that might have a bearing on each pupil's progress. An OfSTED (2000) publication suggests several groups that may be distinguished when considering educational inclusion:

- pupils with SEN
- girls and boys
- minority ethnic and faith groups
- travellers
- asylum seekers and refugees
- pupils who need support to learn English as an additional language
- children 'looked after' by the local authority

- gifted and talented pupils
- sick children
- young carers
- children from families under stress
- pregnant schoolgirls
- teenage mothers
- pupils at risk of disaffection and exclusion.

If there is a worry that some of these groups of pupils are not 'included' in the school's ethos and learning as much as they could be, then the educational concern is that they will not attain or progress well. In order to test whether this is so, schools may examine attainment and progress data of each of these groups and consider how it compares with that of other pupils.

What is suggested in this chapter is that similar analyses are carried out in relation to pupils with SEN. For example, taking the group of pupils identified as having SEN it can be established how the attainment and the progress of pupils within the cohort who are from an ethnic minority group compares with that of pupils who are not. Similarly, the attainment and progress of girls with SEN can be compared to those of boys with SEN.

In the subsequent sections, I look at the examples of reading standards in relation to gender and at numeracy standards with regard to ethnicity. The approach can be adapted to apply to other school subjects, for example science, information and communications technology, design and technology and so on.

A different approach is used when one considers development in other areas such as standards in personal, social, health and citizenship education. This is illustrated focusing on gender and on pupils with behavioural, emotional and social difficulties.

Standards and progress in reading for pupils with SEN in relation to gender

The data

To examine the data according to gender, using our example of reading assessments, the data is separated between boys and girls and a comparison is made between the relative attainment and progress information. This may be done by looking at the average attainment score for boys and comparing it with girls. This can be done for both dates of testing.

The average rate of progress of the re-testing period can also be compared for boys and girls. All this should of course be informed by the teacher's knowledge of the pupils. Let it be assumed that the data indicates that the rate of progress over time is lower for boys with SEN than it is for girls with SEN.

The assumption is that boys and girls would be likely to progress at similar rates. If this is not happening, then the school seeks possible explanations.

Possible interpretations of the data in relation to gender

There could be many possible explanations if differences are found in reading attainment according to gender. These include:

- resources
- staffing
- preferential attraction of optional activities
- lack of interest or appeal in activities likely to improve attainment.

Reading resources may capture the interest of girls more than boys.

The gender of staff may have an influence. If the staff are all or predominantly female, and the school believes that role models for pupils are influenced by the gender of the staff member and the pupil, this may suggest that boys do not have role models in the school whom they can emulate. This might apply if senior staff or influential staff are female.

The preferential attraction of optional activities that are likely to encourage and improve reading may have an impact. For example, optional lunchtime or out of school clubs that encourage reading (including computer clubs that offer activities relating to literacy) may be attracting more girls than boys.

There may be a tendency for boys to regard reading as an unappealing and uninteresting activity.

Of course, if the data indicated that boys progressed better than girls, all of the above explanation would be considered in relation to this. Once the school has examined plausible reasons for the differences found in the reading progress of boys and girls, it can consider the possible provision and intervention that might narrow the difference by improving the progress of the gender group that were doing less well. It is this that the next section examines.

Possible school responses

The possible responses of the school can be presented in relation to the same issues that were considered to affect attainment and progress:

- resources
- staffing
- preferential attraction of optional activities
- lack of interest or appeal in activities likely to improve attainment.

The school could review the resources it uses, auditing and finding out which are more appealing to boys. It could then plan the relocation of resources or the purchase or loan of other resources to address this issue. This is not to assume gender stereotypes in the interests of boys and girls. It is more to see in reality what interests the particular pupils in a particular school at a particular time and harness this, within the bounds of good educational practice, to improve reading standards.

The long-term staffing policy, within the law on equal opportunities, could aim to recruit more male members of staff, particularly to senior positions. In the short and medium term, the school could ensure that visiting staff and others who work with the school, such as artists, sculptors and storytellers, music groups and theatre performers include male role models. If parents helping at the school are mainly or exclusively mothers, the school could examine ways of attracting fathers.

Turning to the possible preferential attraction of optional activities, the school could consider why out of school or lunchtime clubs for reading attract mainly girls. This will lead to strategies to interest boys in these optional activities. If for example membership is affected by the competing interest in other activities scheduled at the same time, these other activities could be rescheduled for another time.

Finally, the school could look behind boys' lack of interest in activities likely to improve attainment in reading. Initially this could be explored by speaking to a sample of boys and seeking to respond to the reasons that they give. This may reflect resources, the competing interest of other activities, lack of role models in the clubs and other issues raised earlier. There may be other reasons such as low self-esteem related to low standards in reading leading to a vicious cycle of lower attainment.

Standards and progress data in numeracy for pupils with SEN in relation to ethnicity

The data

I wish to examine the data according to ethnicity, using the example of numeracy assessments. The data is separated according to whether the child is from an ethnic minority background or not, and the relative attainment and progress information is then compared. This may be done by looking at the average attainment score of pupils from an ethnic minority background and comparing it with that for pupils who are not. This can be done for both dates of testing. The average rate of progress of the re-testing period can also be compared for the two groups. Let us assume that the data indicates that the rate of progress over time is lower for pupils from an ethnic minority group than for pupils who are not from an ethnic minority group.

The assumption is that pupils from different ethnic groups, that is pupils from an ethnic minority background and pupils who are not, would be likely to progress at a similar rate. If this is not happening, then the school seeks possible explanations.

Possible interpretations of the data in relation to ethnicity

There could be many possible explanations if differences are found in numeracy attainment according to ethnicity. These include:

- resources
- staffing
- preferential attraction of optional activities
- lack of interest or appeal in activities likely to improve attainment.

Numeracy resources may capture the interest of one ethnic group more than another.

The ethnic background of staff may have an influence. The staff may be all or predominantly from one ethnic group. The school may believe that role models for pupils are influenced by the ethnicity of the staff member and the pupil. If so, this may suggest that members of some ethnic groups do not have role models in the school whom they can emulate. This might apply if senior members of staff or/and influential staff are from one ethnic group.

The preferential attraction of optional activities that are likely to encourage and improve numeracy may have an impact. For example, optional lunchtime or out of school clubs that encourage numeracy (including computer clubs that offer activities relating to numeracy) may be attracting disproportionately more members of one ethnic group rather than another.

There may be a tendency for members of one ethnic group to regard numeracy as an unappealing and uninteresting activity.

Of course, if the data indicated that pupils from an ethnic minority group progressed better than other pupils, all of the above explanations would be considered in relation to this. Once the school has examined plausible reasons for the differences found in the numeracy according to ethnicity, it can consider the possible provision and intervention that might narrow the difference by improving the progress of the group that was doing less well, as the next section indicates.

Possible school responses

The possible responses of the school can be presented in relation to the same issues that were considered to affect attainment and progress:

- resources
- staffing
- preferential attraction of optional activities
- lack of interest or appeal in activities likely to improve attainment.

The school could review the resources it uses, auditing those appealing to different ethnic groups and finding out which resources each group would find more appealing. It could then plan the relocation of resources or the purchase or loan of other resources to address this issue. This is not to assume ethnic stereotypes in the interests of pupils from different ethnic groups. It is more to see in reality what interests the particular pupils in a particular school at a particular time and harness this, within the bounds of good educational practice, to improve numeracy standards.

Within the law on equal opportunities, the school could aim to recruit more members of staff from particular ethnic groups, particularly to senior positions. In the short and medium term, the school could ensure that visiting staff and others who may work with the school, such as artists, sculptors and storytellers, music groups and theatre performers, include role models from different ethnic groups. If parents helping at the school are mainly or exclusively from one ethnic group, the school could examine ways of attracting members of other ethnic groups.

Turning to the possible preferential attraction of optional activities, the school could consider why out of school or lunchtime clubs for numeracy attract mainly members of one ethnic group. This will lead to strategies to members of all ethnic groups in these optional activities and retain their membership of them. If, for example, membership is affected by the competing interest in other activities scheduled at the same time, these other activities could be rescheduled for another time.

Finally, the school could look behind the lack of interest in activities likely to improve attainment in numeracy to the extent that these relate to ethnicity. Initially this could be explored by speaking to pupils from different ethnic groups and seeking to respond to the reasons they give. This may reflect resources, the competing interest of other activities, lack of role models in the clubs and other issues raised earlier. General strategies for improving the attainment of pupils from ethnic minorities are outlined in a report by the Office for Standards in Education (OfSTED 2000b).

Personal, social, health and citizenship education and standards

Having looked at examples of interrogating data using the example of reading scores and numeracy scores, the subsequent sections examine the approach in relation to assessments of behavioural, emotional and social development.

The example used in Table 8.2 is the framework for assessing personal, health and social education. Other assessments of development can be used such as those outlined in Chapter 4.

The school has gathered assessments of PSHE and citizenship for pupils identified as having SEN. Repeating the assessment after a period of (in the example) 12 months, a second set of P scores is obtained for the same pupils. By deducting the second score from the first, an indication of progress in terms of P levels is obtained for each pupil.

Next, a broad indication of the attainment of the pupils is obtained by adding the initial P scores and dividing them by the number of pupils to give an average score. The second P scores for each pupil are added and divided by the number of pupils to give the average scores for the second testing. The second average score is deducted from the first average score to give the average progress. Looking at this average of progress, the teacher will be able to see the individual pupils that have progressed

Table 8.2 Performance descriptions on two occasions for pupils aged ten years

Pupil's name	January	January 1 year later	Progress in P levels
David (B)	P4	P4	0
Anne (G)	P4	P5	1
Leanne (G)	P5	P6	1
Poojah (G)	P4	P6	2
Francine (G)	P5	P7	2
Nadim (B)	P5	P6	1
Javid (B)	P4	P5	1
Rocchina (G)	P5	P7	2
Michael (B)	P6	P7	1
Adam (B)	P5	P7	2

less than average or more than average. The teacher's knowledge of the pupils will inform judgements about whether the progress can be considered sufficient and the progress of each pupil might be compared with any targets set for each.

Considering other factors

Following the same reasoning as earlier, the data on P levels can be analysed according to different groups within the group of pupils with SEN. For example, according to gender; ethnicity; main type of SEN; social background and age. I will first consider the example of gender.

Standards and progress data in P levels for PSHCE for pupils with SEN in relation to gender

The data

To examine the data according to gender, using our example of performance descriptors, the data is separated into male and female, and the relative attainment and progress information compared. This may be done by looking at the average P score for boys and comparing it with that for girls. This can be done for both dates of testing. The average rate of progress of the re-testing period can also be compared for boys and girls, all this being informed by the teacher's knowledge of the pupils. Let it be assumed that the data indicates that the rate of progress over time is lower for girls with SEN than for boys with SEN. The assumption is that boys and girls would be likely to progress at a similar rate. If this is not happening, then the school seeks possible explanations such as those illustrated below.

Possible interpretations of the P scale data in relation to gender

There are many possible explanations if differences are found in P scale attainment according to gender. These include:

- resources
- staffing
- preferential attraction of optional activities
- lack of interest or appeal in activities likely to improve attainment.

Resources used in PSHCE may capture the interest of boys more than girls.

The gender of staff may have an influence. If the staff are all or predominantly male, and the school believes that role models for pupils are influenced by the gender of the staff member and the pupil, this may suggest that girls do not have role models in the school whom they can emulate. This might apply if senior and/or influential members of staff are male.

The preferential attraction of optional activities that encourage PSHCE progress may have an impact. For example, optional lunchtime or out of school clubs that encourage pupils to 'join discussions by responding appropriately' (QCA, 2001b, p. 27, Performance Description 5) may be attracting more boys than girls.

There may be a tendency for girls to regard PSHCE as an unappealing and uninteresting activity.

Of course, if the data indicated that girls progressed better than boys, all of the above explanations would be considered in relation to this. Once the school has examined plausible reasons for the differences found in the P level progress of boys and girls, it can consider the possible provision and intervention that might narrow the difference by improving the progress of the gender group that were doing less well. It is this that the next section examines.

Possible school responses

The possible responses of the school can be presented in relation to the same issues that were considered to affect attainment and progress:

- resources
- staffing
- preferential attraction of optional activities
- lack of interest or appeal in activities likely to improve attainment
- teaching styles.

The school could review the resources it uses in PSHCE according to how it interests boys and girls. It could then plan the relocation of resources or the purchase or loan of other resources to address this issue. Within the law on equal opportunities, the school could aim to recruit more male members of staff, particularly to senior positions. In the short and medium term, the school could ensure that visiting staff and others who may work with the school, such as mentors, careers specialists and others particularly contributing to PSHCE, include men. If parents helping at the school are mainly or exclusively mothers, the school could examine ways of attracting fathers.

Turning to the possible preferential attraction of optional activities, the school could consider why out of school or lunchtime clubs encouraging PSHCE attract mainly members of one gender group. This will lead to strategies to include girls and boys in these optional activities and retain their membership of them. If, for example, membership is affected by the competing interest in other activities scheduled at the same time, these other activities could be rescheduled for another time.

Finally, the school could look behind the lack of interest in activities likely to improve attainment in PSHCE to the extent that these relate to gender. Initially this could be explored by speaking to boys and girls and seeking to respond to the reasons that they give. This may reflect resources, the competing interest of other activities, lack of role models in the clubs and other issues raised earlier.

The teaching styles used in PSHCE may be favouring girls over boys and these can be examined to ensure that both boys and girls participate fully. For example, it may be found that boys and girls respond differently to opportunities for discussion, demonstrations, visits, outside speakers, small group activities and so on. If this is so, strategies can be developed to improve the participation of all.

Main learning difficulty: data, issues and responses in PSHCE

The data

Turning to the issue of the pupils' main type of SEN, the data of standards and progress in PSHCE is set out so that the scores for pupils with different main types of SEN can be compared. The data might include the attainment and progress of pupils with behavioural, emotional and social difficulties and compare these with other pupils with SEN.

Assume that the standards and progress for pupils with BESD are significantly lower than those for other pupils with SEN. It could be claimed with some justification that this is self-explanatory. By definition, pupils identified as having BESD find it more difficult than other pupils, including other pupils with SEN to progress in areas where personal and social development is at a premium. Yet the reasons for this in a particular school at a particular time with particular pupils can still be examined with profit.

Possible interpretations of the P scale data in relation to type of SEN

There are many possible explanations if differences are found in P scale attainment according to type of SEN. These include:

- staffing
- preferential attraction of optional activities
- lack of skills in participating generally, particularly exacerbated in subjects where there is debate and discussion.

The skills of staff in managing the behaviour of some pupils with BESD will of course influence the potential success of the pupils in attaining in PSHCE. The pupils' relationships with particular members of staff are also important.

The preferential attraction of optional activities that encourage PSHCE progress may have an impact. For example, optional lunchtime or out of school clubs that encourage pupils to 'join discussions by responding appropriately ...' (QCA, 2001c, p. 27, performance description 5)) may not be attracting pupils with BESD because this is an activity they may find particularly difficult.

There may be a tendency for pupils with BESD to find it particularly difficult to take part in subjects such as PSHCE in which there is much discussion and participation.

Possible school responses

The skills of staff in managing the behaviour of some pupils with BESD and the pupils' relationships with particular members of staff can be optimised without allowing the difficulties of the pupil to limit the range and depth of the curriculum he receives. This might mean the appropriate support of a teaching assistant with whom the pupil has a good relationship, to support the pupil in PSHCE lessons that he or she finds particularly difficult.

Support for optional activities that encourage PSHCE progress such as lunchtime or out of school clubs may also be appropriate for the pupil with BESD, at least until the pupil has begun to develop strategies for coping in such groups.

There may be a tendency for pupils with BESD to regard PSHCE as an unappealing and uninteresting activity. Particular teaching of the skills necessary to participate in PSHCE lessons may help. In general, work on areas such as self-esteem, confidence building, providing opportunities for success and other approaches are likely to help the progress of pupils with BESD in all subject areas including PSHCE.

Case study 6: Analysing attainment and progress data on pupils with SEN to raise standards

Bishop Lonsdale Church of England (Aided) Primary School and Nursery in Derby use PIVATS to assess performance levels. This enables the school to measure and track the progress of those pupils who cannot be tracked by National Curriculum assessments. For example, pupils who are achieving consistently at level W (working towards level 1 of the National Curriculum) for the whole of Key Stage 1 would seemingly be making no progress at all. However, by using PIVATS, the school can measure very small degrees of progress and show added value in terms of teaching and learning in English, mathematics, science and personal, social and health education.

PIVATS is also used to set targets, track progress and recognise areas requiring particular development. This allows the school to map out and fine-tune provision where it is required to help the pupils achieve better. For example, if a particular cohort of children require literacy support to help them develop basic literacy skills, the school can (and does) plan interventions during the school week such as intensive teaching.

Recently, Bishop Lonsdale has begun to map provision across the school. It has carried out an audit of interventions that are in place for various children in different classes and this has enabled the requirements of different groups to be better identified.

Each area of SEN is associated with three 'waves' of intervention as follows.

Cognition and learning difficulties
Wave 1: Differentiated curriculum planning
Wave 2: Early learning support, additional learning support, further learning support, Springboard, talking partners
Wave 3: Intensive teaching with the SENCO.

Communication and interaction difficulties
Wave 1: Differentiated curriculum planning
Wave 2: Daily opportunities to practise speech and language skills with a teaching assistant; play skills.
Wave 3: Speech therapy support to build up a programme; the delivery of the programme by the teaching assistant and the SENCO in five sessions per week.

Behavioural, emotional and social difficulties
Wave 1: Whole school behaviour policy; rewards and sanctions in class
Wave 2: Small group withdrawal weekly to support social skills
Wave 3: Nurturing support through regularly withdrawing the pupil from class to complete tasks with the teaching assistant and the SENCO.

Sensory and physical difficulties
Wave 1: Accessibility of equipment; staff to support this in class
Wave 2: Teaching assistant support for some subjects and areas
of the curriculum such as physical education and
information and communications technology
Wave 3: Individual support programme.

(From information kindly supplied by Bishop Lonsdale Church of
England (Aided) Primary School and Nursery)

Summary/conclusion

This chapter examined how data on the attainment and progress of
pupils with SEN can be informed by other information about the pupils,
using the examples of gender, ethnicity and main learning difficulty. The
case study indicated an approach to using data on pupils with SEN to
inform and monitor the effectiveness of particular interventions.

Thinking points

Readers may wish to consider:

- how data on the progress of pupils with SEN can be interpreted to
  further raise standards, for example by analysing it according to
  other factors that may be having an impact
- how the results of such an analysis might be interpreted in a particular school to help inform evaluations of particular interventions as
  well as reviews of resources, staffing and other matters.

Key texts

Gross, J. and White, A. (2003) *Special Educational Needs: Practical
Strategies for Raising Standards,* London: David Fulton Publishers.
Especially Chapter 6, 'Planning provision – using a provision map'.

Chapter 9

Standards and school provision for pupils with SEN

Introduction

In this chapter I consider the use of data on standards of attainment and progress of pupils with SEN in relation to existing school provision. The chapter looks at the quality of teaching, giving due attention to teaching assistants and to the systems and structures supporting teaching. This leads to an examination of a pupil's access to the curriculum and to the ways in which good teaching enhances it.

School organisation is examined as it applies to staff and pupils. Staff organisation includes roles and responsibilities, staff allocation and in particular the role of the SEN co-ordinator. The organisation of pupils embraces the grouping of pupils within usual class groups, the wider organisation of pupils into sets, bands, streams and other structures, and the degree to which pupils are withdrawn from lessons or are supported in classrooms. Other organisational features are reviewed, such as the allocation of staff and the possible effects on the standards of pupils with SEN.

Some aspects of school life are less under the direct influence of the school yet can still have an impact on the standards of pupils with SEN. Examples which the chapter examines are 'external' professional support and the contribution of parents and other members of the community.

Quality of teaching

The OfSTED model of teaching and its relationship to a pupil's progress and attainment

Among the models of what constitutes good teaching is that of the Office for Standards of Education (OfSTED 2003a, b, c) which is based on research into school effectiveness and school improvement. In making their judgements about teaching, OfSTED inspectors consider the extent to which teachers demonstrate certain qualities, skills and knowledge. These include the extent to which teachers:

- show good command of areas of learning and subjects
- plan effectively; with clear learning objectives and suitable teaching strategies
- interest, encourage and engage pupils
- challenge pupils, expecting the most of them
- use methods and resources that enable all pupils to learn effectively
- make effective use of time and insist on high standards of behaviour
- make effective use of teaching assistants and other support
- where appropriate, use homework effectively to reinforce and extend what is learned in school
- promote equality of opportunity.

(e.g. OfSTED 2003a, p. 60)

With regard to the teacher's command of areas of learning and subjects, inspectors judge teachers' knowledge by, among other things, 'how well they are able to cater for the more able and those special educational needs' (ibid., p. 65). In connection with teachers' planning for lessons, inspectors assess the extent to which it 'gives support staff a good framework for adapting the work and modifying approaches for individual pupils with SEN or disabilities' (OfTED 2003a, p. 66). When judging how well teaching 'meets the needs' of pupils with SEN, inspectors 'look for its effect on learning'. Work should be 'matched to pupils' needs and inspectors should be able to see how pupils are making *progress*' (OfSTED 2003a, p. 69, italics added). The OfSTED Handbooks make explicit the rather obvious but important link between teaching and learning, stating that 'learning is the outcome of effective teaching and support combined with pupils' qualities and attitudes' (e.g. OfSTED 2003a, p. 70).

The Teacher Training Agency Standards for Professionals and their relationship to SEN

The *National Standards for Special Educational Needs Co-ordinators* (TTA 1998) sets out:

- the core purpose of the SENCO
- the key outcomes of SEN co-ordination
- professional knowledge and understanding

- skills and attributes; and
- key areas of SEN co-ordination.

In many parts of the document there are references to meeting needs, with no indication of what this would mean or how it would be known if the needs were met. Elsewhere, however, there are more purposeful references to standards and access.

The core purpose of the SENCO is to 'bring about improved standards of achievement for all pupils' (ibid, p. 5).Among the key outcomes for SEN co-ordination are that pupils with SEN, 'show *improvement* in literacy, numeracy and information technology *skills*' (ibid, p. 4 section 2 (a), italics added). Teachers should have 'high expectations of pupils' *progress*' and teaching assistants should help pupils to 'maximise their levels of *achievement* and independence' (ibid., p. 6, italics added).

With regard to professional knowledge and understanding, the SENCO should comprehend 'the main strategies for improving and sustaining high standards of pupil *achievement*' (ibid., p. 8, italics added).

Key areas of SEN co-ordination include that SENCOs 'support staff in understanding the learning needs of pupils with SEN and the importance of *raising their achievement*' (ibid., p. 12, italics added). SENCOs should also 'support the development of improvement in literacy, numeracy and information technology skills as well as *access* to the wider curriculum' (ibid., p. 13, italics added).

Four key areas of SEN co-ordination are set out:

- strategic direction and development of SEN provision in the school
- teaching and learning
- leading and managing staff; and
- efficient and effective deployment of staff and resources.

Strategic direction and development include the need for the SENCO to support staff in understanding 'the importance of raising … achievement' (ibid, p. 12, section 5Aii). The SENCO also advises the head teacher and governors on the level of resources needed to, 'maximise the achievements of pupils with SEN' (ibid, p. 12 section, 5Av).

The document *Qualifying to Teach: Professional Standards for Qualified Teachers Status and Requirement for Initial Teacher Training* (TTA 2002a) sets out the values, knowledge and understanding, and the teaching to be demonstrated for a teacher to be awarded qualified teacher status (QTS). The requirements include that teachers demonstrate 'That they have high expectations of pupils; respect their social, cultural, linguistic, religious and ethnic backgrounds; and are committed to raising their educational *achievement*' (ibid., Chapter 1, section 1, italics added).

The *Induction Standards for Newly Qualified Teachers* (TTA 2002b) sets out requirements that have to be met if a newly qualified teacher (NQT) is to participate successfully in the induction process and complete it. The Standards include that the teacher should, by the end of the induction period, demonstrate that they:

> ... take responsibility for identifying appropriate monitoring and assessment strategies to evaluate pupils' progress and use this information, along with other performance data, to improve their own planning and teaching and *raise the achievement* of boys and girls from all ethnic groups.
>
> (ibid., section (h), italics added)

While there is an emphasis on raising achievement in both the *Professional Standards for Qualified Teacher Status* (TTA 2002a) and the *Induction Standards for Newly Qualified Teachers* (TTA 2002b), too often, when they refer to pupils with SEN, they refer to 'meeting needs'. Implications for pupils with SEN for both the *Professional Standards for Qualified Teacher Status* (TTA 2002a) and for the *Induction Standards for Newly Qualified Teachers* (TTA 2002b), are discussed in detail elsewhere (Farrell 2003a).

In the *National Special Educational Needs Specialist Standards* (TTA 1999), the core standards refer to the development of literacy, numeracy and information and communications technology (ICT). The skills and attributes required of teachers working with pupils with severe or complex SEN indicate the importance of raising standards of pupil achievement.

Teaching assistants

In assessments about the quality of teaching, the contribution of teaching assistants is important. Teachers assume overall responsibility for pupils' learning but part of the OfSTED judgement on good teaching is that teachers 'make effective use of teaching assistants and other support' (e.g. OfSTED 2003a, p. 60). Among factors that tend to improve the quality of the shared teaching task are that the teachers share learning objectives for pupils with the teaching assistant and that the teachers also share planning and monitoring of pupils.

In the *Professional Standards for Higher Level Teaching Assistants* (Teacher Training Agency 2003), higher level teaching assistants are expected to demonstrate certain professional values and practice; knowledge and understanding; and teaching and learning activities.

The knowledge and understanding includes that teaching assistants must 'demonstrate sufficient knowledge and understanding to be able to help the pupils they work with make progress with their learning'. This relates to a specialist area which may relate to 'pupils with particular needs' (ibid., section 2, introduction). Teaching assistants meeting the standards must show they 'know the legal definition of Special Educational Needs (SEN), and are familiar with the guidance about meeting SEN given in the SEN Code of Practice' (ibid., section 2, paragraph 8).

The teaching and learning activities required should take place under the direction and supervision of a qualified teacher in accordance with arrangements made by the school's head teacher. They include that the teaching assistant should 'promote and support the inclusion of all pupils in the learning activities in which they are involved' (ibid., 3.3.3).

The link between teaching and standards of pupils' attainment

The link between higher quality teaching, higher standards of attainment and better progress of pupils will be apparent. Good teaching leads to better learning. Evidence that learning has taken place includes that the pupil makes good progress and reaches higher standards of attainment.

Linking quality of teaching and curriculum access

Access to the curriculum involves ensuring that what is offered to pupils is, as far as can be reasonably expected, taken up by them. A key part of this is through the use of teaching methods that enable all pupils to learn effectively. This involves matching the work closely to the prior attainment of pupils, otherwise known as 'differentiation'.

Differentiation is centrally related to differences in attainment. It concerns the closest matching of activities and the capabilities of pupils. Differentiation is a planned process of organisation and intervention in the classroom aiming to ensure that school work is well matched to the individual characteristics of the pupils.

The effectiveness of differentiation can be judged according to its impact on the standards of attainment reached by all pupils including pupils with SEN.

Systems supporting and enhancing the quality of teaching

The activity of teaching is not solely the task itself but also the structures that surround and support it. For example, agreed planning systems may involve ensuring that long- and medium-term curriculum and subject plans include tasks and assessments enabling pupils with SEN to reach the learning objectives required.

A related way in which systems support teaching is by ensuring that the resources required for teaching are at least sufficient in quality and quantity. This may mean for some pupils with SEN the use of specialist resources such as computer programmes supporting writing and reading. Yet another is the system of monitoring the effectiveness of teaching and ensuring that teachers are aware of the weaknesses and strengths of their teaching. Teachers may be given written reports of their teaching with strengths and weaknesses clearly articulated, and including targets for improving the weaknesses and sustaining the strengths. Reaching these targets may involve support and training, and perhaps the provision of physical resources.

All such support systems can be judged according to their effect on the standards of pupil attainment.

In performance management, teachers' career progress and their pay may be informed by the progress made by the pupils they teach.

Comparing teaching provision

If the data collected on the attainment of pupils with SEN is comprehensive, comparisons can be made of the progress of pupils according to the main teacher working with them. With younger children in primary school, where pupils spend much of the day with the same teachers, comparisons can be usefully made. For example the progress of a small group of pupils with SEN taught by one teacher can be compared with that of other pupils with SEN taught by another teacher providing the pupils have similar types of SEN and start from a similar assessment baseline. With small numbers, such an approach would not be statistically robust, but comparisons may be instructive if they have the confidence of the two teachers involved and are used as possible ways to improve teaching and attainment.

In upper primary school and in secondary school where pupils tend to be taught by many teachers, other comparisons can be made. The progress of pupils with moderate learning difficulties who appear to have equal difficulties in numeracy and literacy could be compared in these two areas of the curriculum. If progress in the two areas was different, this could be explored. Also, the general progress of pupils with SEN could be tracked to see which pupils were progressing satisfactorily and which were not, and why.

All these approaches are not necessarily intended to lay blame at a teacher's door. But they can identify in the same way as for pupils in general what works well for pupils with SEN and what does not. It essentially involves making use of data in a similar way as for all pupils, but with the focus on the cohort of pupils that have SEN, or a group with a particular type of SEN.

School organisation

Staff and pupils

Through the organisation of its staff and pupils, the school increases or decreases its ability to raise the standards of pupil attainment. Part of staff organisation concerns the roles and responsibilities of staff, including their communications. The organisation of pupils refers to the grouping of pupils within usual class groups and the wider organisation of pupils into sets, bands, streams and other groupings.

Staff roles and responsibilities

An underlying principle in teaching pupils with SEN is that of providing a greater level of support to those considered to have the greater 'need'. A manifestation of this is that the school aims to set up systems to ensure that staff with the greatest level of skill or expertise are deployed with the pupils who most require them.

In England, it is expected that the class teacher of a pupil will make the initial judgement about whether a pupil has SEN. While this may appear daunting, particularly for the newly qualified teacher, in each school the presence of the SENCO, having particular expertise in SEN, acts as a safeguard and in practice helps less experienced staff with their decisions. From the earliest indications of SEN, the class teacher may consult with the SENCO for advice, support and practical help. If the pupil does not make expected progress, the SENCO becomes progressively more involved. Should the closer involvement of the SENCO not improve progress, outside support may be called on as necessary. Also, greater amounts of time can be allocated to pupils requiring greater support. In brief, the intention is to enhance the likelihood of attainment being raised by focusing increasing levels of time and expertise on the pupil according to his lack of progress.

Some difficulties in staff allocation

Sometimes schools may focus very well on allocating extra time to pupils with SEN, but may not always ensure that staff with sufficient expertise or experience are regularly working with the pupil. The increasing use of teaching assistants for pupils with SEN is subject to this weakness.

Many teaching assistants work with individual pupils and small groups for a considerable part of the pupil's timetable. They often provide a valuable contribution to the pupil's education. But where teaching assistants are inappropriately or ineffectively deployed, the child can effectively be denied the teacher's skills and knowledge. At the same time the teacher can be gradually losing the skills he has in educating pupils with SEN.

This can be particularly marked in the case of pupils with behavioural, emotional and social difficulties (BESD). The pupil may become increasingly dependent on the individual teaching provided by the teaching assistant and become less and less able to respond in a class setting. Simultaneously, the teacher may be losing skills in dealing with difficult behaviour. The pupil's level of attainment including the development of personal and social skills may consequently be lowered.

One response is to ensure that the teacher as well as the teaching assistant devotes sufficient time to pupils with SEN. Also, teacher and assistant should have sufficient time to share planning based on clear learning outcomes. The teachers can monitor whether these learning outcomes are achieved in the lesson.

Pupil organisation

Preamble

As noted earlier, the organisation of pupils refers to the grouping of pupils within usual class groups and the wider organisation of pupils into sets, bands, streams and so on. This includes the degree to which pupils are withdrawn from lessons or are supported in the classroom.

Whole school organisation

The effect of the school's organisation into structures such as sets and streams may be monitored for all pupils. It may become clear that a judgement about setting is improving overall standards. However, the same analysis that is commonly done for all pupils is not always carried out with particular regard to pupils with SEN as a group where the effects on standards of organisational structures may not be the same as they are for all pupils taken together.

It may be that the effects of an organisational feature beneficial to the progress of most pupils are detrimental to the progress and standards of pupils with SEN. If so, the reasons can be explored and action taken to maintain the possible positive effects on the standards of most pupils, while at the same time ensuring that standards for pupils with SEN improve too.

Classroom organisation

If pupils are withdrawn from the classroom for support, the effects of this on the standards and progress may be monitored and compared with those of pupils with similar types of SEN and starting from a similar baseline of prior attainment who have been supported within classes.

The reasons for any differences in progress can be hypothesised and possible rearrangements to the existing systems may be made using evidence from the school and its own particular circumstances.

The use of standards and progress data in relation to teaching and school organisation

Perhaps the most useful approach to using standards and progress data to appraise school organisation is through benchmarking attainment and progress with schools having a similar and comparable group of pupils with SEN. The similarity is based on the schools having a similar cohort of pupils with SEN. If it is found after a specified period of, say, a term, that one school is enabling the pupils with SEN to make better progress and reach higher standards of attainment than the other school, then each school can explore why.

Finding a similar group is not of course an exact science. But schools are often able to find, sometimes with guidance and information from the LEA, pupils that are comparable as a group. It is important that any comparisons have the confidence of staff, otherwise the potential for what can be learned from comparisons is limited. Such pairing of schools is ideal if they are physically not too far away from each other, enabling senior staff to meet perhaps once a term to review progress.

This might lead to a review of the quality of teaching in the school that is doing less well with pupils with SEN and to a review of its organisational arrangements for pupils with SEN. There are several approaches the school can take towards the latter. The training of staff can be reviewed to ensure that all have the requisite skills and knowledge in relation to SEN. The degree to which pupils are withdrawn from lessons and receive support in lessons can be considered and compared between the two schools. The response of the school will depend on the outcomes of this review.

Professional support

To some degree, professional support to the school can be assessed, refined and improved by using data on the attainment and progress of pupils with SEN. Depending on its exact remit, the work of an educational psychologist, a SEN specialist teacher, behaviour support staff, therapists and others, can be viewed in terms of its contribution to raising the attainment of pupils with SEN in academic, personal and social development.

The work of an educational psychologist can be taken as an example. A report on their current role and future aspirations sets out their 'core functions' which include working with pupils either individually or in groups, and working with schools (DfEE 2000). It was ascertained that schools want, among other things, school-based work in behaviour management. LEAs want psychologists to provide preventative work to avoid social exclusion. Within all this, it is possible to identify ways of working that often raise pupils' attainment.

For example, consider that an educational psychologist is supporting a school implementing a behaviour modification programme for pupils with behavioural, emotional and social difficulties. It is reasonable to consider the effectiveness of the support in terms of its impact on the personal and social development and the behaviour of the pupils concerned. This is not of course to ignore the school's responsibility to implement a programme. Nor is it to seek to blame someone from outside the school if results are not as envisaged. It is by prior agreement to try to determine what has worked well and what can be done better.

If interventions appear ineffective, possible questions for the school to explore are as follows:

- Do other professional partners share the school's awareness of the task of raising the attainment of pupils with SEN?
- Are all partners aware of the range of approaches used by the school to raise the attainment of pupils with SEN, and of the contribution that they might make?
- In relation to standards of pupils' attainment, can the support or advice that was offered be assessed in terms of value for money?
- How long do members of school staff spend working with partners and does the 'return' justify the time?

Having considered these questions, the school may be uncertain of the value of the interventions. If it is judged that, in circumstances when it should, the contribution of professional support colleagues is not sufficiently raising pupil's attainment, there are a variety of school responses.

- All partners can be made more aware of the range of approaches used by the school and of the contribution that they might make as colleagues.
- The school can seek to agree on the strategies, including teaching and learning strategies that will raise attainment.
- If value for money is low, the school can consider using other sources of support and advice that might offer better value.
- The school can consider whether the time spent by its teachers and others working with partners can be reduced and still lead to the same results, thereby improving value for money.

Naturally, it does not have to be only the school that considers matters from this perspective. Supporting professionals may seek to evaluate their contribution in terms of its effect on raising standards of attainment. These professionals and the schools with whom they work may then develop a shared perspective that could be expressed in a service level agreement.

Parents

Parents make important contributions to raising standards of attainment. They may be involved in the school's target-setting process for their son or daughter and may contribute to the achievement of the targets through supporting the pupil's work carried out at home. School–home agreements or contracts can help clarify the respective roles of teachers and parents in this area.

Parents may also give crucial support in helping a pupil reach a behavioural target. Of course, it is a valuable motivating factor for a pupil to see parents and the school working closely together for their benefit.

Where parents help in the school, for example by hearing children (including pupils with SEN) read, the school may wish to provide training to ensure that such help is as effective as it can be.

The community

The community is perhaps best viewed as a body to which the school belongs and from which the school, as part of this community, can often draw goodwill and support. Links with the community, including higher education and business, can be viewed as a given good but can also be informed by their effect on pupils' attainment. Links with local universities or colleges of further education may be used to recruit mentors for some pupils with SEN who would be likely to benefit. Business contacts may include links with companies who could provide resources for pupils with SEN at a very competitive rate of fee. The effect on standards should be traceable, if only in a fairly anecdotal way. It may be evident that some resources, whether human or physical, have had more impact than others.

Questions arising may include the following:

- Are the learning resources that did not work well effectively targeted, appealing and motivating?
- What distinguishes mentors and other outside helpers that are successful with pupils with SEN and those that are not?

This information might be used to:

- feed comments back to companies to improve the appeal and interest of their learning resources
- inform the recruitment and in-school training of volunteers including mentors.

A school policy on SEN

A school policy on SEN should include information on the standards of pupils and progress that they have made. In this way it can be a tool for co-ordinating and evaluating the various contributions to raising standards.

For example, it could summarise the target-setting data and report on the extent to which targets have been reached. If a new intervention is being implemented, this will take on particular significance in that it will to some extent be an evaluation of the effectiveness of the intervention. Such an intervention might be the introduction of a reading recovery programme, the introduction of new physical resources, or extra time allocated to more staff.

National initiatives and their local impact

Attempts have been made to raise the attainment and achievement of pupils (as well as fulfil other aims) through various national initiatives that are expressed through regional or local structures. Some initiatives have particular relevance to raising the attainment and achievement of pupils with SEN.

Early Years Development and Childcare Partnerships seek to bring together early years education and social care through inter-agency planning. Health Action Zones and Education Action Zones co-ordinate action on social disadvantage and additional support for pupils with SEN within a framework often including private sector help.

The Sure Start initiative provides universal services for children under four and their families in disadvantaged communities (www.surestart.gov.uk). The programme seeks to improve the health and well-being of children and their families so children can thrive when they reach school. Sure Start offers parents, and would-be parents, family support; advice on nurturing; health services; and early learning. It may include outreach visiting; support for families and parents; support for childcare, learning and play for children; primary and community healthcare and support for children with SEN including help accessing specialist services. Sure Start offers the opportunity to interrelate family policy and early identification and the support of pupils with SEN particularly in disadvantaged communities.

The Excellence in Cities programme (EiC) was introduced in 1999 to address the issue of low standards in many city schools (Department for Education and Skills, 2002). In EiC action zones, schools and others collaborate to target additional resources on shared problems. Learning mentors form a single point of contact for accessing community and business programmes (such as out of school study support) and for accessing specialist support services such as social and youth services, education welfare services, and careers services. School-based learning support units working on behaviour and basic skills with disruptive pupils at risk of exclusion provide separate short-term teaching and support programmes and many work closely with learning mentors and out of school support services. Beacon schools in EiC areas aim to contribute to raising standards through disseminating good practice, and through some schools offering advice on SEN.

The Learning and Skills Council (LSC) is responsible for developing, planning, funding and managing post-16 education and training, except higher education, and work-based training for young people. In England, the LSC has local bodies which are responsible for raising standards and 'securing provision to match local learning and skills needs'(DfES 2001a, 10.18). In meeting its responsibilities, the Council must have regard to the needs of people with learning difficulties. It must take account of the assessments of people with learning difficulties arranged by the Connexions Service. The Council seeks to make sure that young people with learning difficulties or disabilities have access to high quality learning.

SEN regional partnerships have encouraged discussion of issues concerning the provision of particular groups of children (Department for Education and Skills/Department of Health, 2002, pp. 74–5). The partnerships bring together LEAs, local health and social services and the voluntary and private sectors. One of these partnerships is the London Regional Partnership mentioned in the case study in Chapter 3.

Summary/conclusion

This chapter considered the use of data on standards of attainment and progress of pupils with SEN in relation to existing school provision. I looked at the quality of teaching, giving due attention to teaching assistants and to the systems and structures supporting teaching. This led to an examination of a pupil's access to the curriculum and to the ways it is enhanced by good teaching.

School organisation was examined in relation to staff and pupils. Staff organisation included roles and responsibilities, staff allocation, and in particular the role of the SEN co-ordinator. The organisation of pupils embraced the grouping of pupils within usual class groups, the wider organisation of pupils into sets, bands, streams and other structures, and the degree to which pupils are withdrawn from lessons or are supported in classrooms. Other organisational features were reviewed such as the allocation of staff and the possible effects on the standards of pupils with SEN. The chapter examined 'external' professional support and the contribution of parents and other members of the community.

Thinking points

Readers may wish to consider:

- as part of school self-evaluation, systematically examining the contribution to raising standards of attainment and achievement for pupils with SEN of a range of factors including the contribution of staff, the curriculum, school organisation and professional support.

Key texts

Farrell, M. (2003) *The Special Education Handbook* (3rd edition), London: David Fulton Publishers

The range and variety of staff, curriculum aspects, school organisational influences and professional support from which schools and others can review in terms of the contribution to raising standards is indicated in the thematic index of the *Handbook*.

Chapter 10

The special school and other specialist SEN provision

Introduction

The Labour government's attempts to explain their approach to special schools has included supposing that there are strong moral reasons why pupils with SEN should be educated 'with their peers' (DfES 1997, p. 43) while still envisaging that parents will have a continued 'right to express a preference for a special school' (ibid., Chapter 4). More recently, the foreword to the *Report of the Special Schools Working Group* stated 'The special school sector enjoys the Government's full support' (Special Schools Working Group 2003, p. 2).

In this chapter, I will refer to provision in special schools, units for pupils with SEN, pupil referral units educating pupils with SEN and other provision that is mainly separate from mainstream schools as 'specialist SEN provision'. I outline implications for specialist SEN provision of what has been said in this book concerning pupils with SEN. The chapter then considers the *Report of the Special Schools Working Group* (Special Schools Working Group 2003), with particular reference to what is said about standards of attainment and achievement.

Definitions and criteria of SEN and identification and assessment

Definitions of SEN are as relevant to specialist SEN provision as to the mainstream school. Special schools and units are often designated as providing for pupils with particular types of SEN such as severe learning difficulties or behavioural, emotional, and social difficulties (BESD). This is not to ignore that in some special schools and units, the SEN of some pupils is particularly complex and is difficult to describe in terms of a single type of SEN.

Criteria within the parameters of the legal definition of SEN are important in informing the admission arrangements for specialist SEN provision. They may specify the degree of severity or complexity of the type of SEN that would be associated with provision being offered in a mainstream school or in specialist SEN provision. For example, where the level of behavioural, emotional and social difficulty is so severe that the pupil is damaging the education of other pupils in mainstream, specialist SEN provision may be indicated.

Closely related to definitions and criteria is the identification and assessment of pupils with SEN. Specialist SEN provision will almost invariably educate pupils who have statements of SEN although sometimes pupils for whom a statutory assessment is being carried out are also educated in specialist SEN provision.

Curriculum and assessment, and target-setting

In specialist SEN provision, there are tensions around the curriculum. On the one hand, such provision may be expected to provide a broad and balanced curriculum, including the National Curriculum. On the other hand, they may more effectively raise standards of attainment and achievement by focusing on other features. These include:

- the 'access' subjects of English, numeracy, and information and communications technology, which, as well as being important in themselves, allow access to other areas of the curriculum
- personal, social, health and citizenship education.

Similar issues arise with regard to assessment. If the curriculum of specialist SEN provision differs too greatly from that of a mainstream school, then assessments will need to be modified so that they focus on what is taught. For example, if there is a focus on functional skills such as eating, washing and dressing, these will need to be assessed. It is essential that such curriculum developments and assessments are, as far as practicable, dovetailed into the wider agreed National Curriculum for all children.

Within specialist provision, it is not always easy to compare the attainment of pupils meaningfully, for example to develop benchmarking to inform target-setting. Among the reasons for this is that different specialist SEN provision may have similar designations but not have similar pupils.

Consider two special schools in different areas, both providing for secondary-aged pupils with BESD. In one local area there may be a unit for pupils with BESD in one or more mainstream schools, a pupil referral unit which provides for pupils including those with BESD. The LEA may also have a policy of placing some pupils with very severe BESD in residential special schools. In the second area, there may be no pupil referral unit, no units for pupils with BESD in mainstream schools and no policy to place pupils in residential special schools.

Given all this, the severity and complexity of the BESD of pupils in the special school in the second area is likely to be higher than that of pupils in the special school in the first area. It would take particular care therefore to compare the progress and attainment of their respective pupils if the two schools were to work together for benchmarking.

Some practical examples will indicate ways in which target-setting is being tackled.

In a primary-aged specialist SEN provision for pupils with severe learning difficulties (SLD) and profound and multiple learning difficulties (PMLD) targets are set according to the percentage of pupils reaching specified steps of progress using the P scales. Pupils are first considered as being on upper, middle and lower bands of attainment.

A specialist SEN provision for pupils with SLD/PMLD sets targets in terms of the percentage of pupils achieving a specified accreditation (including the Award Scheme and Development Accreditation Network or ASDAN assessments) and in terms of improved attendance.

A specialist SEN provision for pupils of primary school age with moderate learning difficulties (MLD) sets targets relating to the National Curriculum levels. This involves the percentage of pupils achieving level 2 of the National Curriculum (that is what is achieved by a typical pupil aged seven years old) at the end of Key Stage 2 (when the pupil is 11 years old).

A provision for pupils of secondary school age with MLD sets targets in relation to the percentage of pupils achieving one or more General Certificate of Secondary Education (GCSE) qualifications at grades A* to G.

A primary provision for pupils with BESD sets targets for the percentage of pupils in year 6 achieving level 4 and above at the end of Key Stage 2 (when a pupil is 11 years old). The provision is aware of its very small cohort of pupils. The school considers it more relevant to use the results of standardised reading and numeracy assessments taken by all pupils to set targets in terms of year by year increases in knowledge and skills.

In a secondary provision for pupils with BESD, targets are set according to the percentage of pupils achieving one or more GCSEs and according to the percentage who achieve Certificates of Educational Achievement that underpin GCSEs.

Inclusion and the role of specialist provision

Education in specialist SEN provision, especially the special school itself, has been recently viewed in different lights by the Government.

On the one hand the 'Green Paper', *Excellence for All Children: Meeting Special Educational Needs,* stated there are 'strong educational as well as social and moral grounds for educating children with SEN with their peers' (DfEE 1997b, p. 43). It was not specified what these grounds were. What was so offensive about this to many staff working in specialist SEN provision was what it appeared to imply if pupils were not educated with their age 'peers'. This was that something was being done that was against the child's educational and social interest and it was against some moral precept. At the same time, the document recognised the continuing need for special schools to provide for a very small proportion of pupils whose 'needs' could not be fully met in the mainstream.

On the other hand, the foreword to the *Report of the Special Schools Working Group* indicates that 'The special school sector enjoys the Government's full support' (Special Schools Working Group 2003, p. 2).

In part because of the increased interest in that aspect of inclusion arguing for fewer or no pupils in what it sees as 'segregated' provision, the role of specialist SEN provision has come under critical scrutiny. In this light, it is particularly important that the role of specialist SEN provision is fully understood and agreed, at least locally. This can help with making fair judgements about the continuation and evolving role of such provision on educational grounds, and not according to any political ideology. Standards of attainment have a role to play in these judgements (Farrell 2000).

A more balanced and informed view of specialist SEN provision than is sometimes expressed is likely to appear when two developments occur. Firstly, supporters of full inclusion will need to recognise the work of good specialist SEN provision. Secondly, anyone wishing to see such provision continue on ideological grounds rather than on merit will come to see that special SEN provision must continue to earn its place in the range of effective educational provision.

As indicated in Chapter 6, standards of attainment can be used to inform judgements about the appropriateness or otherwise of educating pupils in a mainstream school or in specialist SEN provision. It is essential therefore that staff working in specialist SEN provision, staff working in mainstream schools, parents and others know what standard of attainment is reached by the pupils in different settings so that these can be compared with similar pupils.

An important role for staff working in specialist SEN provision is to identify with others the pupils in the school who will benefit most from spending proportions of time in a mainstream school. The proportion of time can be increased or decreased according to the progress a pupil is making in the mainstream school. To risk being repetitious, this of course includes progress in personal, social, emotional and behavioural development as well as in cognitive development. In particular, a special school may have close links with a unit in a mainstream school educating pupils with the same type of SEN (for example speech, language and communication difficulties). These links can act as a bridge to aid the gradual transfer of pupils from special to mainstream school classrooms or vice versa, informed by the progress pupils make and the standards they achieve.

Funding

Being an expensive form of education makes it important that specialist SEN provision can demonstrate the progress that it enables pupils to make and the levels of attainment pupils can reach from a known baseline. Their contribution as a centre for training staff, for physical resources and advice, as well as for outreach work, and so-called 'in reach' work also adds to the value for money that specialist SEN provision can give.

The use of standards and progress data with pupil information

The analysis of standards and progress data and pupil factors may include gender, ethnicity, main learning difficulty, social background and age. All of these apply to analyses in specialist SEN provision. In the case of some particular SEN, the interpretation of data requires particular caution. For example, gender may be related to the SEN. Three times as many boys as girls are identified as having autism while Rhett Syndrome and Turner's Syndrome affect girls only.

The specialist SEN provision can make particular note of the progress of groups amongst its pupils. For example, in a provision for pupils with SLD, a smaller group of pupils having autism might be identified, or others who have particular difficulties with communication, and their progress monitored. The progress and attainment of these pupils would be compared with that of other pupils to look for possible inconsistencies and to seek further improvements in provision.

The use of standards and progress data to improve provision

The quality of teaching in specialist SEN provision can be judged using such criteria as those in the OfSTED framework. It can be evaluated according to the progress of pupils in different class groups so long as it is clear that the comparisons are justifiable and fair.

Turning to curriculum access, specialist SEN provision may educate pupils with a particular type of SEN such as a hearing impairment. Nevertheless pupils may start from a different baseline of attainment, meaning it is important to differentiate their work. The organisation of staff and pupils is as important in specialist SEN provision as it is for pupils with SEN in mainstream school and all can be informed by monitoring pupils' standards and progress.

The contribution of lay support and of outside professional support can be similarly evaluated with reference to its impact.

The *Report of the Special Schools Working Group*

This section examines the *Report of the Special Schools Working Group* (Special Schools Working Group 2003), with particular reference to what is said about standards of attainment and achievement.

The report states that it 'sets out a vision for the future role of special schools within the overarching framework of inclusion, and maps out a programme for change' (ibid., p. 5). The definition of inclusion is restricted to 'the Government policy which places emphasis on children and young people with SEN being educated in mainstream schools, rather than the wider definition of broader social inclusion' (ibid., p. 14). But inclusion is 'not just about the type and place of school, but about the wider inclusion experiences which **all** children with SEN are entitled to expect' (ibid., p. 7 bold in original).

Among the key principles it considers should underpin change is 'to have high expectations of all pupils with SEN, to raise levels of attainment and achievement' (ibid., p. 5).

Considering teaching and learning, the report recognises that 'It is important to have robust mechanisms in place to allow all schools to monitor the progress made by pupils with SEN' (ibid., p. 34). A case study of The Bridge School, a special school in Telford, refers to teachers in the school completing a 'unit specific attainments comment' at the end of a lesson (ibid., p. 35). Another case study concerning St Margaret's School in Tadworth refers to learning support assistants being responsible for 'maintaining records of one or two pupils' progress against targets in each session' (ibid., p. 39).

Regarding funding and structures, the report discusses different ways in which special schools should work in future: twinning model, federations and clusters. Federations are described as special schools working with mainstream schools to 'raise attainment for all the pupils' and it is said that Government is keen to support schools including special schools to federate and 'to develop joint structural approaches to raising standards of teaching and learning' (ibid., p. 59). Mention is made of the collegiate academies project in Birmingham in which some of the collegiates involve a special school and structures are being developed 'to enable special schools to work in a more collaborative way with a view to raising standards for all pupils' (ibid., p. 59). Similarly, in Portsmouth, a number of head teachers including head teachers of special schools 'have taken joint responsibility for raising standards for all pupils' (ibid., p. 59).

A focus group for professionals informed the working groups' deliberations. Regarding inclusive learning, there was a need 'to better understand how children learn ... in order to better help them to learn – thus raising levels of attainment and achievement' (ibid., p. 102). There is a need to accept that 'pupils do not make the best progress when they are treated uniformly' (ibid., p. 102).

It was stated that 'standards should be considered in the broader sense of achievement with recognition that progress that may not always be quantifiable will still be valid' (ibid., p. 108). Also, 'good teaching and access to teaching styles were keys to raising standards in both mainstream and special school although models may be differentiated in each case' (ibid., p. 108). Ongoing assessment was 'a useful tool in measuring small step achievement' (ibid., p. 109). There was 'a paucity of evidence in terms of national data/published research to highlight achievement among children with SEN' (ibid., p. 109). There was a concern that 'attainment is all about upward progression' (ibid., p. 109). Also, 'measuring progress against National Curriculum levels is not always appropriate for some pupils with SEN, the progress of the individual is more important. For example progress in mobility or independence which could not be measured against the targets in the IEP' (ibid., p. 109).

The affective domain should be recognised 'so as to enable pupils to progress – dignity, confidence and emotional well-being are crucial' (ibid., p. 109). Special school PANDAs were 'not helpful in accessing levels of attainment' (ibid., p. 110). An issue 'in relation to measuring progress' was that 'if a school doesn't do well against the P scales, is that because they under-performed or because the original assessment assumed a higher level of performance or under-estimated the level of special need?' (ibid., p. 110). Professionals were 'unable to make year on year comparisons on progress, but nationally, there should be data setting out movement on P-scales from one key stage to the next' (ibid., p. 110).

Key messages from focus groups involving parents and young people, also set up to inform the Working Group, included that 'All were equally committed to a positive focus on access and achievement for all pupils across the education system' (ibid., p. 123). Also, 'Parents and young people have stressed the importance of valuing and progressing the potential and achievements of pupils with special educational needs or disabilities' (ibid., p. 124).

The parents had ambitions for their children 'in terms of educational achievement, social inclusion and what one parent described as: active citizenship, being part of and contributing to the community, all the ordinary important things which other people expect as of right' (ibid., p. 127).

Looking to the future, pupils were 'keen to have their aspirations and progress recorded, recognised and celebrated' (ibid., p. 170).

The references in the report indicate the importance in special education of standards, progress, attainment and achievement within the context of inclusive learning.

Summary/conclusion

This chapter outlined implications for specialist SEN provision of what had been said earlier in the book concerning pupils with SEN. It considered the *Report of the Special Schools Working Group* (Special Schools Working Group, 2003), with particular reference to standards of attainment and achievement.

Thinking points

Readers may wish to consider:

- the extent to which in any particular LEA there is a shared understanding between mainstream schools, specialist provision and others of the role and future of specialist provision.

Key text

Farrell, M. (2004) *Special Educational Needs: A Resource for Practitioners,* London: Sage/Paul Chapman
Chapter 4, 'Political judgements, inclusion and the future of special schools', considers factors that might determine political judgements about the future of special schools. This includes the context of international reports on inclusion, the *Report of the Special Schools Working Group* (Special Schools Working Group, 2003), parental views and the relative achievement of pupils in particular mainstream and special schools.

Bibliography

Barber, M. (1997) 'Target-setting and school improvement – the way forward: A letter to all chief education officers in England,' 21 July

Booth, T. and Ainscow, M. with Black-Hawkins, K. (2000) *Index for Inclusion: Developing Learning and Participation in Schools,* Bristol: Centre for Studies for Inclusion in Education

Bracknell Forest Local Education Authority (2002), *Bracknell Forest Borough Council Revised Criteria for Carrying Out Statutory Assessments of Special Educational Needs, Drawing Up Statements of Special Education Needs and Ceasing Statements of Special Educational Needs*, Bracknell Forest LEA

Clarke, C., Dyson, A. and Millward, A. (eds) (1995) *Towards Inclusive Schooling,* London: David Fulton Publishers

Coopers and Lybrand (1996) *The SEN Initiative: Managing Budgets for Pupils with Special Educational Needs,* London: Coopers and Lybrand

Department for Education and Employment (1997a) *Excellence in Schools,* London: *DfEE*

Department for Education and Employment (1997b) *Excellence for All Children: Meeting Special Educational Needs,* London: DfEE

Department for Education and Employment (1998) *Supporting the Target Setting Process: Guidance for Effective Target setting for Pupils with Special Educational Needs,* London: DfEE

Department for Education and Employment (1999a) *The National Curriculum Handbook for Primary Teachers in England,* London: DfEE

Department for Education and Employment (1999b) *The National Curriculum Handbook for Secondary Teachers in England,* London: DfEE

Department for Education and Employment (1999c) *Circular 10/99: Social Inclusion – Pupil Support,* London: DfEE

Department for Education and Employment (1999d) *Circular 11/99: Social Inclusion – The LEA Role in Pupil Support,* London: DfEE

Department for Education and Employment (2000) *Educational Psychology Services (England): Current Role, Good Practice and Future Directions – Report of the Working Group,* London: DfEE

Department for Education and Employment (2001) *Supporting the Target Setting Process: Guidance for Effective Target setting for Pupils with Special Educational Needs (Revised March 2001)*, London: DfEE

Department of Education and Science (1978) *Special Educational Needs: Report of the Committee of Enquiry into the Education of Handicapped Children and Young People (The Warnock Report)*, London: Her Majesty's Stationery Office

Department for Education and Skills (2001a) *Special Educational Needs Code of Practice*, London: DfES

Department for Education and Skills (2001b) *Inclusive Schooling: Children with Special Educational Needs* London, DfES

Department for Education and Skills (2002a) *Key Stage 3 National Strategy: Designing the Key Stage 3 Curriculum*, London: DfES

Department for Education and Skills (2002b) *Excellence in Cities: Schools Extending Excellence – Annual Report*, London: DfES

Department for Education and Skills (2003a) *Data Collection by Type of Special Educational Needs*, London: DfES

Department for Education and Skills (2003b) *Excellence and Enjoyment: A Strategy for Primary Schools*, London: DfES

Department for Education and Skills (2004a) *The Management of SEN Expenditure*, London: DfES

Department for Education and Skills (2004b) *Removing Barriers to Achievement: The Governments' Strategy for SEN*, London: DfES

Department for Education and Skills/Department of Health (2002) *Autistic Spectrum Disorders: Good Practical Guidance-01-Pointers to Good Practice*, London: DfES/DoH

Donovan, N. (ed.) (1998) *Second Chances: Exclusion from School and Equality of Opportunity*, London: New Policy Institute

Farrell, M. (2000) 'Educational inclusion and raising standards', *British Journal of Special Education*, 21(1), 35–8

Farrell, M. (2003a) *Understanding Special Educational Needs: A Guide for Student Teachers*, London: RoutledgeFalmer

Farrell, M. (2003b) *Special Education Handbook* (3rd edition) London: David Fulton Publishers

Farrell, M. (2004a) *Special Educational Needs: A Resource for Practitioners*, London: Sage/Paul Chapman

Farrell, M. (2004b) *Inclusion at the Crossroads: Special Educational Needs – Concepts and Values*, London: David Fulton Publishers

Farrell, M., Kerry, T. and Kerry, C. (1995) *The Blackwell Handbook of Education*, Oxford: Blackwell

Fletcher-Campbell, F. (1996) *The Resourcing of Special Educational Needs*, Slough: National Foundation for Educational Research

Gartner, A. and Lipsky, D.K. (1989) 'New conceptualisations for special education', *European Journal of Special Needs Education*, 4(1), 16–21

Gross, J. and White, A. (2003) *Special Educational Needs: Practical Strategies for Raising Standards*, London: David Fulton Publishers

Kilfoyle, P. (1997) *Every Child is Special: Proposals to Improve Special Needs Education*, London: Labour Party

London SEN Regional Partnership (2004) *Joint Criteria for Statutory Assessment of Special Educational Needs*, London: London SEN Regional Partnership

Morris, E. (2002a) *Insight Pre-School: Assessing and Developing Self-esteem in Children Aged 3–5*, Windsor: NFER-Nelson

Morris, E. (2002b) *Insight Primary: Assessing and Developing Self-esteem in Children Aged 5–11*, Windsor: NFER-Nelson

Morris, E. (2002c) *Insight Secondary: Assessing and Developing Self-esteem in Young People Aged 11–16* Windsor: NFER-Nelson

Office for Standards in Education (1996) *Setting Targets to Raise Standards: A Survey of Good Practice*, London: Office for Standards in Education/ Department for Education and Employment

Office for Standards in Education (1999) *Inspecting Schools 3–11: Guidance for Inspectors and Schools*, London: OfSTED

Office for Standards in Education (2000a) *Evaluating Educational Inclusion: Guidance for Inspection of Schools*, London: OfSTED

Office for Standards in Education (2000b) *Raising the Attainment of Ethnic Minority Pupils: School and LEA Responses*, London: OfSTED

Office for Standards in Education (2003a) *Handbook for Inspecting Nursery and Primary Schools*, London: OfSTED

Office for Standards in Education (2003b) *Handbook for Inspecting Secondary Schools*, London: OfSTED

Office for Standards in Education (2003c) *Handbook for Special Schools and Pupils Referral Units*, London: OfSTED

Office for Standards in Education (2003d) *'Notes of Guidance' for completing forms S1 and S2 relating to school inspection, September*, London, OfSTED

Office for Standards in Education (2003e) *Excellence in Cities and Education Action Zones: Management and Impact*, London, OfSTED

Office for Standards in Education (2004) *Setting Targets for Pupils with Special Educational Needs HMI 751*, London: OfSTED

Peer, L. and Reid, G. (2003) *Introduction to Dyslexia*, London: David Fulton Publishers

Qualifications and Curriculum Authority (2001a) *Planning, Teaching and Assessing the Curriculum for Pupils with Learning Difficulties: English*, London: QCA

Qualifications and Curriculum Authority (2001b) *Planning, Teaching and Assessing the Curriculum for Pupils with Learning Difficulties: Mathematics*, London: QCA

Qualifications and Curriculum Authority (2001c) *Planning, Teaching and Assessing the Curriculum for Pupils with Learning Difficulties: Personal, Social and Health Education and Citizenship*, London: QCA

Qualifications and Curriculum Authority (2001d) *Supporting School Improvement – Emotional and Behavioural Development,* London: QCA

Rouse, M. and Agbenu, R. (1998) 'Assessment and special educational needs: Teachers' dilemmas', *British Journal of Special Education,* 25(2), 81–7

Rouse, M., Shiner, J.G. and Danielson, L. (2000) 'National assessment and special education in the United States and England and Wales', in M.J. McLaughlin and M. Rouse (eds), *Special Education and School Reform in the United States and Great Britain,* London: Routledge

Schools Curriculum and Assessment Authority (1997a) *Value Added Indicators for Schools,* London: SCAA

Schools Curriculum and Assessment Authority (1997b) *Target Setting and Benchmarking for Schools: Consultation Paper,* London: SCAA

Special Schools Working Group (2003) *Report of the Special Schools Working Group,* London, Department for Education and Skills

Teacher Training Agency (1998) *The National Standards for Special Educational Needs Co-ordinators,* London: TTA

Teacher Training Agency (1999) *The National Special Educational Needs Specialist Standards,* London: TTA

Teacher Training Agency (2002a) *Qualifying to Teach: Professional Standards for Qualified Teacher Status and Requirements for Initial Teacher Training,* London: TTA

Teacher Training Agency (2002b) *Induction Standards for Newly Qualified Teachers,* London: TTA

Teacher Training Agency (2003) *Professional Standards for Higher Level Teaching Assistants (September 2003),* London: TTA

Wade, J. (1999) 'Including all Learners: QCA's approach', *British Journal of Special Education,* 26(2) 80–2

Ware, J. (2003) *Creating a Responsive Environment for People with Profound and Multiple Learning Difficulties,* London: David Fulton Publishers

Index